Self-Initiation

for the

Solitary Witch

Attaining Higher Spirituality
Through a Five-Degree System

D1522651

Self-Initiation
for the
Solitary Witch

Attaining Higher Spirituality
Through a Five-Degree System

By

Shanddaramon

This edition first published in 2004 by New Page Books, an imprint of Red Wheel/Weiser, LLC
With offices at:
65 Parker Street, Suite 7
Newburyport, MA 01950
www.redwheelweiser.com
www.newpagebooks.com

ISBN: 978-1-56414-726-4
Library of Congress Cataloging-in-Publication Data
Shanddaramon, 1959-
    Self-initiation for the solitary witch : attaining higher spirituality
through a five-degree system / by Shanddaramon.
        p. cm.
    Includes index.
    ISBN 1-56414-726-6 (pbk.)
        1. Witchcraft. I. Title.

    BF1566.S44 2004
    133.4'3—dc22

                                                            2003070226

Cover illustration and design by Jean William Naumann
Interior by Kristen Parkes

Printed in the United States of America
IBI
10 9 8 7 6 5 4 3 2 1

This book is dedicated to all those spiritual seekers

who have the courage to follow their own path to the true,

the right, the good, and the beautiful.

Acknowledgments

I wish to thank all those people who helped to make this book a reality. I would like to thank my first teacher, Enosdeval, for starting me out on this path. He taught me that the light of the path is in your own heart, and he had the patience to wait around until I finally got it. I would like to thank my partner, Mary, for her endless support. Thank you to all the people of our first teaching circle—the Unified Pagan Community of Central Vermont—for providing a space in which to talk, laugh, and experiment through all the principles developed in the creation of this work. I thank Lady Leeannanshea for first sparking my curiosity in this path and teaching me some very valuable first lessons. I would also like to thank my students of Clan Tynwald and of the Sacred Order of Living Paganism (especially my first student, Dan) who I often think have taught me much more than I have offered to them.

Contents

Preface

How This Book Came to Be

I began as a solitary Wiccan under the guidance of a patient and trusting teacher. I later became an initiate in a local coven that was just beginning to form. I found the coven experience to be unsatisfying. The controlling hierarchy of a single priestess felt restricting and uncomfortable to my free, searching spirit. I enjoyed finding my own way without being told exactly what I had to learn, study, and believe. After all, I had left the traditional religions for that very reason. I was also appalled by the behavior of some of those who called themselves High Priests and Priestesses. With very little study and training, they led a group of people and dictated their spiritual lives to others, oftentimes with little idea of the consequences of their actions. More often than not, I found myself questioning their sense of social and group responsibility. Like any religious tradition, the responsibility of leadership requires careful training and learning. I and several other members of the coven left and began our own study group in order to help each other learn and grow together in the Craft—each in our own directions, but working together.

I was very much attracted to Wicca for its love of the earth and her cycles and for the sense of ritual that the path provides. The idea that each person is encouraged to find an individual path appealed to me. Most of all, I began to study Wicca because it was meaningful to me while still being fun. "Why can't a religion be both?" I asked. After more than a year of detailed study of Wicca, Paganism, occult studies, and the practices of ancient mystery schools, I devised my own degree system. Several members of the Pagan study group I helped start in Vermont worked with me to create this system and began working on its path as well. Thus, we created a new system of learning outside of the traditional coven.

I offer this degree system to others who may be practicing alone or within a Pagan study group and who may want an idea of some of the things that can be learned for personal development in the Wiccan tradition. Each person should feel free to develop his or her own degree system and to add to or delete from any item in this book. This work is simply a guide that may offer ways to create a personal study program. It is not a cookbook to be followed word for word. Use it as you see fit to create a path of personal and spiritual growth. Most of all, allow the work you do to be for your own spiritual development. It is from following your own path that you will discover the true inner joy of spirituality.

How to Use This Book

In Hellenistic Greece and, most likely, far earlier in history, there existed several mystery schools. These spiritual schools existed, in theory at least, to teach people about the Great Mysteries of the gods. This learning took place in stages or degrees. Students began by dedicating themselves to a particular school of study. With each successive degree, the initiate delved into a deeper and more profound learning of these mysteries. This book brings the learning style of the mystery school to the path of the practitioner of Wicca. It divides intense learning and practice into five different degrees.

Each chapter discusses a level in detail and contains a listing of the degree associations, a list of goals, a discussion of the focus of each level and its related Great Mystery, and a detailed explanation of each step in the degree, followed by a brief review. For each degree there is a color, title, prefix, number, and a list of goals. The seeker may use these as needed. For example, the color could be used for the decoration of a robe, belt, or pendant to indicate to others the degree earned. The title can also indicate your level. The prefix can be used when referring to your name (common or magickal), and the number can refer to the level of the path. As always, these trappings are to be used only if doing so appeals to you. For those who do not wish to wear robes, pendants, or fancy belts, or who do not wish to discuss or share with others their progress, these adornments are pointless. If, however, they create a sense of fun and mystery for the seeker, then use them in this manner—for fun is a great part of this religion. Using any of these items to differentiate you from others solely for the purpose of elitist fancies is against the theme of this path. Constant vigilance against this attitude is necessary for the dignity of this tradition. More than that, however, is the fact that such arrogance is a hindrance in spiritual development.

Each chapter also includes several charts, graphs, and tables to help you understand the concepts discussed. These are listed as Items and are numbered. These Items should be transferred to your journal or collection of notes (such as a Book of Shadows) so that you will have a quick and easy reference as you continue to study.

Each of the degrees also suggests that the seeker perform a final ritual. These rituals can be as simple or as complex as desired, and may be enacted singly or with a group of people that support such an activity. It is important to mark one's progress, and such rituals are a fitting and meaningful way to do so. The first ritual that will be introduced will be the Dedication ceremony. Strictly speaking, this ceremony will not be a full-blown Wiccan ritual because little of the ritual practice will have been learned at this point. It will, instead, be a simply designed ceremony. Learning how to do rituals will be a main focus of early development, and the initiation ritual practiced at the end of every degree is a good way to practice and refine what has been learned. I recommend that each degree take a minimum of a year and a day of study, but you will be able to best determine your own rate of development.

Introduction

What Is Wicca?

Wicca is a Pagan (earth-centered) religion that respects, honors, and worships the natural forces of the earth and the universe through ritual and personal relationships. Representations of these cosmic forces can be worshipped through the dual deities of God and Goddess in whatever form or fashion the individual practitioner prefers. The strength of Wicca is that it is not solidly fixed in form. Nor should it ever be. Creativity and individual expression are important parts of the practice and should always be honored and encouraged.

Specifically, most Wiccans believe in the following concepts:

- A respect and reverence for nature and all her cycles with an ongoing observance of those cycles through joyous celebratory rituals.
- An understanding of the division of the one power of the universe divided into two forces: masculine energies represented by the God and feminine energies represented

by the Goddess. (Some also recognize a third entity called the Child.)

- A belief that the physical world in which we live is not the only reality and that not only do other realms exist, but they may be explored and used.

- A belief in reincarnation—that we can learn from past-life experiences and that what we do now affects future-life experiences.

- A belief in the power to focus and direct energies of the will to enact necessary change. (This practice is often called magick.)

- A belief in free will and choice with an understanding of the responsibilities and consequences of such freedom.

- A respect and tolerance for all sacred paths and practices that cause no harm to others and the ability to incorporate other sacred rituals, teachings, and deities into personal practice when desired.

- A thorough understanding and application of the Wiccan Rede and the Threefold Law to daily life.

Let's look at each one of these concepts in detail:

A respect and reverence for nature and all her cycles with an ongoing observance of those cycles through joyous celebratory rituals.

This means that Wicca is first and foremost a practice that celebrates, honors, and respects nature. This does not mean that all Wiccans live in a Thoreau-style shack in the woods. This would be impractical for many. (Practicality is another feature of Wiccan practice.) It does mean that Wiccans respect and revere nature as a sacred living presence. Earth and all that exist upon her are alive and are worthy of respect. We try to live with nature and do not believe that this planet was provided for our private use to destroy and alter as we see fit. To maintain a connection with nature, Wiccans celebrate her natural cycles through rituals such as *sabbats*, *esbats*, and *astors*. The solstices and equinoxes are four of the eight sabbats or holidays (holy days) that Wiccans celebrate. Days that are approximately equidistant in time from these are the four high sacred days of Wicca, bringing the total number of sabbats to eight. Each sabbat celebrates both the reality of natural cycles and the mythologies of life and rebirth associated with those cycles. The eight sabbats and their general dates (though not always exact) of observance are:

- ◆ Yule—December 21 (Winter Solstice).
- ◆ Imbolc—February 1 (height of winter).
- ◆ Ostara—March 21 (Spring Equinox).
- ◆ Beltane—May 1 (height of spring).
- ◆ Litha—June 21 (Summer Solstice).
- ◆ Lughnasadh (Lammas)—August 1 (height of summer).
- ◆ Mabon—September 21 (Fall Equinox).
- ◆ Samhain—October 31 (height of fall).

Wiccans also celebrate the cycles of the moon. Each full moon is celebrated in a ritual called an esbat. Our tradition also celebrated the dark of the moon in a ritual called an *astor*—a word that means star. Our main symbol, the pentagram, is a five-pointed star, and, at the time of the dark moon, we are able to see the stars more clearly.

An understanding of the division of the one power of the universe divided into two forces: masculine energies represented by the God and feminine energies represented by the Goddess.

This means that Wiccans honor and worship not just one solitary god figure, but two complementary deities called the God and the Goddess or sometimes the Lord and the Lady. Some believe that the Lord and Lady were created as complementary pairs from a single force or entity. Some simply call this entity the Great Mystery or The One, while others call her the Great Mother Goddess or the Great Spirit. She is great because she is beyond human comprehension. She is Mother because from her all things were "born." She is the Goddess because she is a great nurturing wisdom. This does not necessarily mean that she is seen as a giant floating woman in the sky. These are terms that help to create a relationship with something more mysterious than we can imagine. This personal relationship with the energy of the cosmos is important to the Wiccan. From the Great Mother Goddess or Spirit came the complementary forces of God and Goddess. The God is often represented as the horned god of old. He represents male energies, while the Goddess represents female energies. She is the goddess of the earth and of love. Some will honor the God and Goddess strictly by those names, while others may use names from ancient religions or mythologies to provide a system of deities such as those from Celtic, Norse, or Egyptian practices.

The High Priestess of the coven in which I began my studies taught me about a third deity called the Child. This deity has not been introduced in many traditional Wiccan practices, but I have found it to be a strong influence in my own. This deity represents life itself and the Great Mystery of things unknown. All of life is the great Child for which the God and Goddess provide and nurture. The God represents or embodies (depending on your perspective) male forces in the universe, while the Goddess represents or embodies female forces. The Child represents the neutral force, which can embody both male and female aspects. That is the essence of life. All life embodies both male and female characteristics. Like the baby of a family, the child is the one that continues the energies of the parents into the future. The parents have created a child, but it is also the child that defines the parents, for two people cannot be called parents if there is no offspring. That which is true for earthly parents is true for the gods. "As above, so below." This is what is celebrated in the deity called the Child.

A belief that the physical world in which we live is not the only reality and that not only do other realms exist, but they may be explored and used.

This means that Wiccans believe that this realm of physical existence is not the only realm in which we exist. We live day to day in a physical reality to be sure, but we are more than physical beings. We also possess emotions and are capable of thought. Emotions and thoughts are not things that can be pointed to and touched as physical realities, but they are as real as any physical object and they are important components of living. Thoughts and emotions are just two examples of things that do not exist as physical objects. There are many other things that Wiccans say coexist with the physical, and Wiccans believe that these realms, through practice, can be accessed and used to improve one's life and the lives of others.

A belief in reincarnation—that we can learn from past-life experiences and that what we do now affects future-life experiences.

The cycles of the earth and the moon are seen as proof from the Goddess that there are no complete endings—all things are renewed. This includes one's own life. Just as the new moon grows to full strength then wanes only to become another new moon, so does the life of the individual go through a cycle of rising strength, gradual decay, and eventual rebirth. Wiccans believe, in one fashion or another, that each life is a culmination of lives from the past. No life is a single entity in the never-ending dance of life and death. We can learn from those lives that came before us, and what we do in this life affects many lives after our own. Living in this way demands that you consider carefully the past and that you take responsibility and care for what you do with your life in the present.

A belief in the power to focus and direct energies of the will to enact necessary change.

This is an acceptance of the fact that all things, all matter, are energy. Wiccans believe that there are many different forms of energy that exist within us and within the universe itself. These energies are real and can be experienced. They can also be accessed and manipulated (within the bounds of natural laws). The ability to work with energy in this manner is often called magick. (The "k" was added to the original word by Aleister Crowley who distinguished illusionary magic as performed by stage magicians from the type of magick we are discussing.)

A belief in free will and choice with an understanding of the responsibilities and consequences of such freedom.

This means that Wiccans believe that each person is free to choose for him- or herself what to believe and how to live. We do not believe that life is controlled or influenced by a jealous god nor by a manipulating entity called the Devil (in fact, Wiccans do not even believe in the Devil). Instead, each individual is a free agent who makes choices based on personal beliefs and individual relationships to the deities. This also means that Wiccans recognize that each individual is responsible for his or her own decisions and actions.

A respect and tolerance for all sacred paths and practices that cause no harm to others and the ability to incorporate other sacred rituals, teachings, and deities into personal practice when desired.

To me, this is one of the great strengths of Wicca and one that sets it apart from many other religions. Many of the world's religions suffer from an attitude of intolerance, which has caused great strife in the world. Wicca is different. It recognizes that each person is unique and needs to worship in his or her own way. No religion or spirituality is considered wrong so long as its philosophy or practice does not include harm to self or others. Many Wiccans incorporate ideas from other religions into their own practice and respect all others to find their own way.

A thorough understanding and application of the Wiccan Rede and the Threefold Law to daily life.

The Wiccan Rede and the Threefold Law are the primary components of ethical practice for the Wiccan. A simple version of the Rede states, "As it harms none, do as you will." This relates to the earlier discussion of the concept of free will. Wiccans believe that we are each free to do as we please so long as what we do does not harm other living things. This includes other people, animals, and any other being, including yourself. This means more than just considering what harm may be involved in personal decisions or actions. Wiccan ethics also warns that all actions result in consequences. Wiccans believe that the energy used to take an action is returned to you. More than that, the resulting return of energy is multiplied three times. This is known as the Threefold Law. The Threefold Law simply stated says that whatever you do will be returned to you threefold. This concept causes us to consider carefully the consequences of each action. These two concepts will be discussed in more detail in the section concerning ethics (page 67).

The Five Elements and the Five Degrees

Another belief that nearly all Wiccans share is the concept of the five elements, which represent forces in life. These elements are Air, Fire, Water, Earth, and Spirit. These forces were once believed to be the actual building blocks of all creation. Modern Wicca understands these elements to represent many forces that exist in life.

The five degrees developed throughout this book are based on the five elements of Wicca. The five-pointed star of Wicca, called the pentagram, represents each of these.

Five Elements on a Pentagram

The equilateral cross also represents these five elements, which is the essence of the Wiccan altar and the magick circle. Though the order and placement of the elements within this cross can be any way you like, the traditional placement is used here.

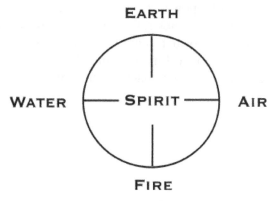

Placement of Elements

There are many correspondences to these elements, but the ones that concern us here for the sake of personal development are those that relate to the five elements of humanity. Those are the mind (the seat of the intellect—related to Air), the heart (the seat of the life force and outer emotions—related to Fire), the soul (the personal connection to the spirit and inner emotions—related to Water), the body (the physical—related to Earth), and the spirit (the eternal essence that is part of each of us—related to Spirit). Each of these five human elements is related to the five basic elemental forces.

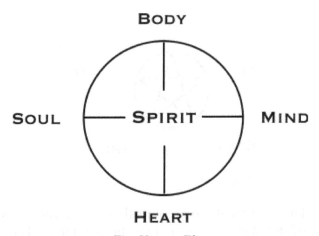

Five Human Elements

It is also traditional in Wiccan practice to create circles of power and protection. To invoke power, the circle is created in a clockwise fashion. (Clockwise is sometimes referred to as *deosil*.) Banishing is enacted by going in the opposite direction (referred to as *widdershins*). We begin in the center, move forward, and then proceed clockwise around the circle and then return back to the center.

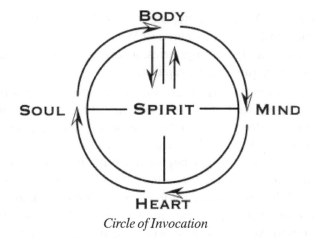

Circle of Invocation

The five levels of attainment used in this book follow this path of invocation.

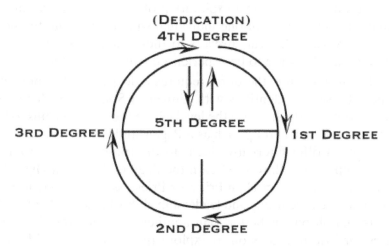

Path of Invocation

Before beginning on the first level, the seeker dedicates him- or herself to a course of study. The act of Dedication is represented symbolically in the North—the realm of the physical. Here, the seeker makes a physical commitment to learning through the act of Dedication. For the first degree, the seeker must learn a great deal of information and, thus, moves symbolically to the East—the realm of the intellect. After learning, the seeker then puts the information into practice and earns the degree of Wiccan Practitioner. Before one can delve into the deeper mysteries, a certain amount of background information is required for preparation.

The second degree is sought in the realm of the emotions, symbolized by the element of Fire in the South. This is the realm of action and learning by doing. Completing the second degree, the successful seeker earns the degree of Wiccan Priest. It is in seeking the second degree that the practitioner begins the pursuit of the Great Mysteries. The ancient Greek Mystery schools taught their initiates the Great Mysteries of the universe in gradual stages. While seeking the second degree, the practitioner will begin a search for the answer to the first of three Great Mysteries. This will be a uniquely personal journey, for the answer to these Mysteries must be found and explored solely by the individual. Why were these Mysteries kept so secret? It was because revealing the answers to someone else denied that person the opportunity for a personal exploration of discovery and because the unique understanding of one individual will not translate to another through words. The true answers to these Great Mysteries are beyond words. They are to be experienced from deep within.

The next degree, the third, requires a deeper level of practice in which the seeker identifies with Universal Spirit through the individual soul (West). It is also the level where the seeker begins to learn to work and lead a group such as a Pagan study group or a *coven*. (In this book, I offer alternative ideas to the traditional coven.) Those who complete the third level earn the degree of Wiccan High Priest or Priestess. The term High Priest or Priestess is used only to recognize a degree of learning and leadership ability but should not be used to distinguish one as better than another. At this level, the Wiccan Priest or Priestess goes on to explore the second Great Mystery— expanding on the knowledge learned and experienced from the first.

The fourth degree returns the seeker to the realm of the physical (North), but now he or she will learn to merge the physical with all the other parts of the self. The main focus of the fourth degree is the rebirthing ritual. Those who complete this level earn the degree of Wiccan Elder. The rebirthing ritual was the culminating event of the Greek mystery schools. It is during this time that the third and final Great Mystery will be explored. Having delved into these deep Mysteries, the High Priest or Priestess is then ready to be reborn into a new life. The ancient mystery schools would send their initiates into a dark place such as a cave, which symbolized the womb of the earth goddess. After suffering a ritual death, the initiate then experienced rebirth, and emerged from the dark cave into the light of new life. If successful, this activity could become a major life-changing event for the individual.

The final degree, the fifth, is recognition of years of long and hard work. In this degree, the practitioner applies all that has been learned. The seeker learns to live the life of a true Wiccan. After living such a life for 10 years, the Wiccan earns the title of Wiccan Ancestor.

Chapter 1

The Dedication:
Beginning the Journey

⟳

- ⟿ Number: 0
- ⟿ Title: Seeker
- ⟿ Prefix: none
- ⟿ Color: white
- ⟿ Gift: pendant
- ⟿ Goals:
  1. Profess a desire to learn and study the Craft.
  2. Create a Dedication ceremony.
  3. Enact the ritual.

Deciding to become a seeker of spiritual knowledge and experience through a detailed system of degrees is no small undertaking. You are committing yourself to intense personal development over a long period of time. Because this will be your own system, you are free to work at your own pace and can stop anytime without the fear of humiliation from a teacher. However, this fact should not become a reason for taking on this work without conviction. You must first truly decide if you are willing to take on such intense personal study.

If you are, then the next step is to engage in a physical act of Dedication that will signal to yourself (and others, if you wish) that you are serious about taking on this adventure in spiritual growth. The way to do this is through a ritual that marks the beginning of a path of study. The goal of this level is to enact a ceremony of Dedication.

Before you actually dedicate yourself to the Craft, take some time to consider why you wish to begin this work and how you will find time to do it. One important step in any spiritual journey is to keep a journal in which to record your activities and thoughts as you develop. In Wicca, this journal is often called a Book of Days. Why is a journal so important? It is an excellent way of marking your progress. It also forces you to organize your thoughts and can help you to review your day's work. Later on, you will be able to look back on all the work you did and see just how far you have progressed. Make a commitment to write in your Book of Days every day. In it you should include all your personal thoughts about your practice and progress.

The Dedication Ceremony

Your first step on the Sacred Path of Wicca is to dedicate yourself to the work to come. The Dedication ceremony does not need to be a complicated or fancy ritual. In fact, at this level, it should be a very simple and uncomplicated yet meaningful ceremony. Do not concern yourself with proper tools and fancy words unless it is your desire to do so. All these things will be introduced to you later as you progress. For now, we will keep the ceremony very simple. Later on you will learn about all the principles of constructing a detailed ritual, but that is not needed for this basic act of Dedication.

Before you actually begin writing your ceremony, think about what it will mean to you. Think about how you could represent this meaning symbolically. Remember that this is your ceremony and that you can devise it any way you wish. What is important is that it be significant and meaningful to you. Decide if you want this ceremony to take place within a circle of friends or if you want to do it just for yourself. Do you want it to take place indoors or out?

After you have thought through these details, it will be time to write down the actual ceremony. Though all Wiccans practice differently, there are some common elements to their rituals. I offer you here some of the very basic elements of ritual, but you may use as much or as little of these as you desire. Remember, what is important is that you create a ceremony that provides meaning and joy to you.

For a very basic Dedication ritual you should consider the following steps:

1. Prepare yourself.
2. Set up an altar with symbolic images and candles.
3. Devise carefully and announce your intention.
4. Create a sacred space (usually in a circle).
5. Invite the God, Goddess, and Child (or other deities) to the ceremony.
6. Make a statement of Dedication.
7. Thank your deities.
8. Undo your circle.
9. Ground yourself.

Begin by preparing yourself for the ritual both mentally and physically. You might want to take a ritual bath with specially selected herbs or oils, or wear special clothing. Clear your mind of daily concerns and concentrate on your task. If you are at home, make sure you will not be disturbed or interrupted. Next, set up a small table or work area as an altar. Again, we are going for simplicity here, so it need not be particularly fancy unless that is your desire. A simple card table covered with a white cloth would do just fine. Later, you may want to create a permanent altar from which you can work whenever you wish or may want to create an altar that is set up whenever the need arises.

Here are my suggestions for your altar: On the back of your altar, place three candles in holders. On the left-hand side, place a green candle for the Goddess. On the right-hand side, place a red candle for the God, and, in the center of these two but slightly forward, place a purple candle for the Child. This, of course, is how I do it and you are welcome to use any system of placement you wish. If you do not wish to work with any deities either as symbolic forces or as personifications, this is perfectly fine as well. Feel free to adorn your altar with whatever objects or symbols are meaningful to you. First, write down and then announce out loud what you intend to have happen. Doing so makes you think clearly about exactly what you mean to do. This is a very important step in all ritual work.

The next step is to claim a sacred space of your own. This can be done symbolically or through physical objects. You may draw a circle around your work area with chalk, salt, herbs, or a rope, or you can create an invisible barrier. It does not matter. Later, you will learn to create this circle through energy. It is traditional to create this circle in a clockwise fashion (usually starting in the East). When you have accomplished this, call the God, Goddess, and Child (or any other deities) to your circle to witness your ceremony. Again, this need not be complicated unless you want it to be. Light a candle for each as you do so. The burning light of the candle will represent the energy and light of each deity. After you have called in your deities, announce your dedication to study through a simple but meaningful statement. Speak from your heart about what you intend to do and all will be well. For many, a Dedication ritual is a great act of freedom. Having finally found a spiritual path that resonates deep within, some have experienced an overwhelming feeling of joy. If you experience this ecstasy, then honor those feelings and express them. If you feel like singing, dancing, or chanting, then, by all means, follow your heart and dance in the joy of renewal.

To end the ceremony, release your deities (or whatever you dedicated your worship toward). That is, thank them for witnessing your ceremony and ask them to return from whence they came. Snuff out each candle as you go. (Most Wiccans prefer not to blow out candles as this is seen as an affront to the element of Fire and prefer, instead, to use a candle snuffer.) Then, undo your circle in the opposite manner in which you created it.

The final step of doing any ritual is to ground yourself. Even though the ceremony being discussed here is very simple, it is possible that energies were raised during its enactment. (You may be more powerful than you know!) Energies raised within and around the body may be sensed. You may have felt warmth or had tingling sensations. You may have felt a presence or experienced a sensation as if there was electricity in the air. You may have become light-headed or felt a sense of renewed energy as if you had drank several cups of coffee. All of these are possible experiences of sensing energy. It is also possible that you raised energy but did not detect any noticeable change. Regardless of what you may have or have not felt, it is important that you ground those energies and return them back to the earth. Not doing so may leave you feeling restless, listless, or may cause you bodily discomforts such as headaches. One of the best ways to ground yourself is to simply place yourself close to the ground, putting as much contact with your body to the earth as is possible and comfortable. Concentrate on letting any excess energy drain back to the earth. One teacher explains it as if you are watching a glass of water that is filled with sand. Raising energies is like shaking up the glass. The sediment is stirred and whirls about in the water. When you ground yourself, it is like letting the glass sit. Slowly, the sediment slows down and settles to the bottom of the glass. This is the same for you. While touching the ground, allow the energies you have raised to settle to the bottom and back into the earth. When you feel comfortable, relaxed, and balanced, rise up and end your ceremony. The following ritual is a sample of a Dedication ceremony. Use it as an example to create your own ceremony.

Item 1: A Rite of Dedication

Purpose: Use as a guide or inspiration for creating a personal ritual.

1. Prepare your altar and yourself.
2. Make a statement of intent.

    Tonight, I will perform a rite of Dedication to the path of Wicca. I confess that I am ready in mind, heart, body, and soul to begin this journey and that I am dedicated to a higher spiritual awakening.

3. Cast the circle.

    a. Cast a circle around yourself and/or participants.

    Now in this circle rightly spun, a sacred rite is thus begun. May I now be safe and sure for the work I here procure.

    b. Light altar candle to the Goddess.

    O great Goddess of Love, whose feminine energy is symbolized by the silver moon, accept this humble servant who yearns to be recognized as a seeker of your ways. Grant me protection, guidance, and wisdom as I walk this path.

    c. Light altar candle to the God.

    O great God of Light, whose masculine energy is symbolized by the golden sun, accept this humble servant who yearns to be recognized as a seeker of your ways. Grant me protection, guidance, and wisdom as I walk this path.

d. Light altar candle to the Child.

O great Child of Life, whose mysterious energy is symbolized by the twinkling stars, accept this humble servant who yearns to be recognized as a seeker of your ways. Grant me protection, guidance, and wisdom as I walk this path.

4. Enact the ceremony.

I hereby accept the responsibilities inherent in seeking a higher level of study by helping others both within and beyond this circle and by seeking help when it is needed. As a seeker of this path, I vow to honor this and all spiritual teachings. I vow to respect and honor all practitioners I now know or may know of this and all sacred paths. I vow to respect and honor myself as a unique and sacred being. I hereby proudly and without reservation, dedicate myself to becoming a Wiccan Practitioner. From this day hence, I proclaim that I am a Seeker in the Craft of Wicca. For the good of one and all, so mote it be!

a. Place a pendant with a white cord around your neck to symbolize your dedication. Dance, sing, or chant, if you feel moved to do so.

5. Open the circle.

a. Extinguish Child candle.

To the source of creativity, O Child Earth, unnamable entity, hear my words addressed to thee. If you have come to bless this rite, I thank you now for your great light.

b. Extinguish God candle.

To the source of masculinity, O Father Sun, god entity, hear my words addressed to thee. If you have come to bless this rite, I thank you now for your great light.

c. Extinguish Goddess candle.

To the source of femininity, O Mother Moon, goddess entity, hear my words addressed to thee. If you have come to bless this rite, I thank you now for your great light.

    d.   Undo the circle.

        Now this circle I undo for this sacred rite is through. Let these blessings I bestow like a seed, take root and grow. Blessed Be!

  6.   Ground excess energy.

        As above, so below.

Congratulations for taking this important first step! You are now a Seeker of the Craft. When you have completed your ceremony, be sure to mark the date in your Book of Days. Reflect upon the ceremony and consider what worked well and what did not. Take notes on your feelings and impressions about the ritual. All of these thoughts will become important as you learn to build, create, and enact more complicated rituals in the future. Attach a white cord to your pendant that you now wear to symbolize your dedication.

You are now ready to begin work on the first degree.

Chapter 2

The First Degree: Path of the Intellect

- ❧ Number: 1
- ❧ Title: Wiccan Novice
- ❧ Prefix: Maid or Squire
- ❧ Color: yellow
- ❧ Gift: athame
- ❧ Goals:
    1. Explain in writing why you wish to commit to further study.
    2. Start magickal books.
    3. Understand the basic concepts and tenets of Wicca.
    4. Begin study of the Great Wheel.
    5. Study magickal alphabets.
    6. Study the ethical principles of Wicca.
    7. Study the symbolism of Wicca.
    8. Understand Pagan history.
    9. Study other mystical and religious traditions.
    10. Understand and practice the basics of magick, ritual, and spellcraft.

11. Understand and practice the basics of healing.

12. Understand the basics of divination.

13. Write and enact a first degree Initiation ceremony.

The first degree is about learning, and there is much to learn for intellectual understanding is an important first step in development. It is not the only step, but understanding the basic principles of Wicca will guide you as other skills develop. Only when you have a firm grasp of the basic principles and fundamental skills can you begin to explore the Great Mysteries. The goal of this level is to question and learn.

You have now dedicated yourself to continued study of the Craft and should commit yourself to at least a year and a day of work to determine if this is the right path for you. Consider what your goals will be for this degree. Be sure to write these thoughts and ideas into your Book of Days.

Your Magickal Books

You have already begun to work on one of your magickal books— the Book of Days. The book you have started will now be called your Seeker Journal and you should commit to maintaining it throughout your year and a day of study as a seeker. When you decide to begin your work on the first degree, finish your Book of Days and close it out. For each level, you should begin a new journal. Keep your journal with you any time you engage in any activity or practice related to your Wiccan studies.

There is also a second book that you will need to start. Rather than a journal of thoughts, impressions, and recordings of your work, this other book will be a place to record those specific things that you learn. In it, you will store all the information you gain in this level. This book is called a Book of Whimsy (BoW).

The Book of Whimsy is another tradition taught to me by my first High Priestess and may be a new idea to some Wiccans. The BoW is not meant to make the traditional Book of Shadows seem trivial. *Merriam-Webster's Dictionary* defines whimsy as "a fanciful or fantastic device, object, or creation especially in writing or art." This describes the book quite well. Your first book of notes should be fanciful and fantastic. It will be a menagerie of notes that will eventually develop into your first Book of Shadows.

The Book of Whimsy is where you will keep all the notes of your studies. It will be your reference guide for all the things you learn along the way. Sure, you could just refer to all those books you will be reading, but having a central reference from which to access information will be extremely valuable, and the very act of compiling such a book is an important part of the learning process. At this stage, a Book of Whimsy should probably be a loose-leaf three-ring binder into which you can insert different notes and studies. All the things you learn in this level should be recorded in your BoW. You should also consider adding a reading list and a list of terms in your book as you go.

Basic Concepts of Wicca

The Basic Tenets

Let's begin our studies by understanding the basic concepts of Wicca. There are many fine books on the basics of Wicca. Do not limit yourself to just one book, because Wicca is an eclectic and varied path and each practitioner has his or her own personal view. It is important that you create your own view, but first you should understand as many of the views of others as you are able. Try to determine what are the common elements of all Wiccan traditions. Here are some that I have discovered. As with many of the things to which you will be introduced in this section, it is not important that you completely understand every detail of what you are learning, for that will come with application and practice. For now, it is more important that you copy these things into your BoW and learn as you go. This does not mean that you should accept all these things as absolute. Instead, learn them now. Then, later, when you have learned and experienced more, review all these things you have learned and revise them to fit your own experiences. This is one reason why your journal and BoW are so important.

Let's begin by reviewing the basic tenets of Wicca discussed in the Introduction.

Item 2: The Basic Tenets of Wicca

Purpose: To understand some common elements and principles between the many traditions of Wicca.

- ◆ A respect and reverence for nature and all her cycles with an ongoing observance of those cycles through joyous celebratory rituals.
- ◆ An understanding of the division of the one power of the universe divided into two forces: masculine energies represented by the God and feminine energies represented by the Goddess. (Some also recognize a third entity called the Child.)
- ◆ A belief that the physical world in which we live is not the only reality and that not only do other realms exist, but they may be explored and used.
- ◆ A belief in reincarnation—that we can learn from past-life experiences and that what we do now affects future-life experiences.
- ◆ A belief in the power to focus and direct energies of the will to enact necessary change. (This practice is often called magick.)
- ◆ A belief in free will and choice with an understanding of the responsibilities and consequences of this freedom.
- ◆ A respect and tolerance for all sacred paths and practices that cause no harm to others and the ability to incorporate other sacred rituals, teachings, and deities into personal practice when desired.
- ◆ A thorough understanding and application of the Wiccan Rede and the Threefold Law to daily life.

Enter your ideas of the basic tenets of Wicca into your Book of Whimsy. Again, these things may change as you continue, but begin with a base of ideas from which to grow.

The Deities

There has been much discussion of the deities up to this point, and it is time to gain some understanding of this concept within

Wiccan practice. Unlike most religions, Wicca does not demand a singular understanding of the gods upon which all followers must agree and to whom they must swear allegiance. Wicca is very much a personal religion. Each practitioner must develop his or her own personal understanding of and relationship to the gods. For some, the gods are real entities that can be personally felt and understood. To others, the gods are representations of energy forms that make up life and who are worshipped symbolically. Others worship specific gods of other cultures. For example, a practitioner may choose to worship the ancient Egyptian gods as either real entities or as representations of forces and relationships understood from those ancient times. Again, it does not matter, and it is up to you to define your own understanding and the practices you will use to put that understanding into your life.

Many people include in their Book of Whimsy the Charges of the Deities. These are texts that represent an understanding of the deities. For each, the deity calls upon the practitioner to honor and respect their qualities. These charges are often read in rituals that honor that deity. For example, an *esbat* is a ceremony that celebrates the Goddess in her representation of the full moon. During an esbat, some read the Charge of the Goddess. Like everything else, there is no requirement that you use or follow these charges. You can even rewrite them or write your own to suit your own needs. Whichever you choose to do, enter the results into your BoW. The charges (I prefer to name them the Calls of the Gods) in this text are my own and not the traditional ones used by many others.

The Goddess

The Goddess is most often seen as a provider. She can be Mother Earth or she can be represented by the moon. Ancient Celts recognized different aspects of the Goddess as related to the different phases of the moon. For others, the Goddess is the only deity. She is the ultimate reality, and all other deities are from her. Item 3 is my Call of the Goddess.

Item 3: The Call of the Goddess

Purpose: Can be read during esbat rituals. Creates an understanding of the Goddess and how to worship her. Provides a sample of a charge from which an original charge can be written.

Hear the call of the Goddess:

Come together, O followers of the Lady.
Gather round when you are ready
during the nights when the moon is full—
hear my sacred call to you.
Dance and sing all in my name
make love and music all the same;
for I am the essence of femininity.
Joining in love is my affinity.
I am the love that binds all things.
I am the song the lover sings.
Mine is the chalice of the water of life
whose truth washes clean all fear and strife.
Mine is the earth in all its forms.
I am the calm seas as well as the storms.
Let none stop you once you begin
to seek joyous union here and again;
for all these things shall you live and learn
and then to me shall you return.

The God

For many in Wicca, the God is represented as the playful sensual consort of the Goddess. Many relate him to the ancient Greek God Pan. He is the Green Man, the great Hunter, or the Horned One of the woods. He is celebrated during the eight sabbats, or sun festivals. Item 4 is my Call of the God.

Item 4: The Call of the God

Purpose: Can be read during sabbat (sun) rituals. Creates an understanding of the God and how to worship him. Provides a sample of a charge from which an original charge can be written.

Hear the call of the God:

Come together, O followers of the Lord.
Gather round by staff and sword

during the days when the great sun burns
that mark the seasons when the Great Wheel turns.
You shall gather as the ancients do
to learn my sacred call to you.
Let your bodies bask in my heat.
Make glad your hearts and merry meet;
for I am the essence of masculinity,
growth in the light is my affinity.
I am the light within all that lives.
I am the joy that love gives.
Mine is the blade that cuts false from true;
pointing the way for the light to shine through.
Mine is the flame of the dancing fire.
I am the heart that burns with desire.
Let none stop you from shining bright.
Let one and all bring forth inner light.
For all these things shall you live and know
and come through me to fully grow.

The Child

The Child is the sum total of all life. It is the energy of life and it is what helps us to become who we are. It is given to us without discrimination. No one creature is more blessed than another. It is also not our own, for we are brought to life with it and then it is taken away so that a continuous renewal—the great dance of life—can continue. Our great spiritual journey is to use this energy of life to its fullest to realize our potential, to experience life while we can, and to come to understand, appreciate, and worship its source. We are the living light of this energy, and it is our purpose in life to mentally, emotionally, spiritually, and physically shine that light as bright as possible.

Item 5: The Call of the Child

Purpose: Can be read during astor rituals. Creates an understanding of the Child and how to worship it. Provides a sample of a charge from which an original charge can be written.

Hear the call of the Child:

Come together, O followers of the Child.
Gather 'round without want or wile.
During the nights when the dark moon is nigh,
when the stars shine bright within the sky,
you shall let love and trust ensue
as you hear my call to you.
Enjoying in full measure the life you lead,
take full well this gift of life decreed;
for I am the essence of sacred mystery.
The dance of life is my affinity.
I am revealed in the unraveled fear
like the twinkle of stars that in dark appear.
Mine is the silence from which all sound begins.
I am that which never begins nor ends.
Mine is the center of the turning wheel—
the inner essence that is forever still.
Let none stop you from seeking silence.
Let none sway you from inner guidance.
So long as harm shall not be sent
Live through me in full intent.

The deities represent (or take form) as opposing properties that seek to be balanced. Because they are in constant motion, temporary imbalances occur, but the tendency is to seek a natural harmony. In some cases, the Child is the third element that makes balance possible. Item 6 lists some of the properties of each deity.

Item 6: Deity Properties

Purpose: To understand the interaction of energies between the gods. To view how these energies interact in life. To be able to seek balance by observing opposite forces in nature.

	God	Goddess	Child
Cosmic Body	sun	moon	stars
Direction	ascending	descending	stationary
Guiding Spirit	wisdom	compassion	patience
Action	receiving	giving	maintaining
Force	active	retroactive	stillness
Gender	male	female	androgynous
Personality	animus	anima	both
Thought	analysis	synthesis	creation
Cosmic Energy	time	space	space/time

The Elements

An important concept to understand in the Craft of Wicca is the concept of the five elements consisting of the four Classical elements and the fifth element—Spirit. Ancient philosophers understood some or all of these elements as being the actual building blocks of the universe. This is not the case for most Wiccans. Instead, the four Classical elements (Earth, Air, Fire, and Water) and their correspondences represent four energy forces that exist in all things. What we currently understand as the actual basis of reality is energy and matter (which, of course, is energy in a much slower state). The dance of life is the constant transformation of energy to matter and matter to energy.

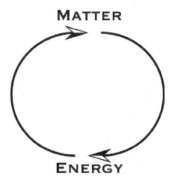

Dance of Life

In between these states are the transitional states of being. Energy condenses itself into a form we call matter, and matter dissipates to become energy.

These four states of energy in transition are represented by the four elements and can be related to other foundations. Take physics, for example. Modern physics points out that there are four energies present in the subatomic world, and they exist to hold and interact with other particles. These forces are the strong nuclear force, the weak nuclear force, electromagnetic energy, and gravity. Each of these could be said to be represented by the four elements. Another example is the four aspects of humanity: The intellectual, the emotional, the spiritual, and the physical parts of each of us could be represented by the four elements. The most obvious correlation is with the four compass points: North, South, East, and West. These relationships are an important part of Wiccan ritual design.

The elements are the foundation of life. Without them, life would have no place to exist. The traditional four elements are Air, Fire, Water, and Earth. It is important that you understand the representative qualities of each, for they will become important tools in your understanding and development of the Craft. In the previous example, each of the four elements represents the four states of energy. Earth represents matter. Air represents the transition from matter to energy. Fire represents energy and Water represents the transition from energy to matter.

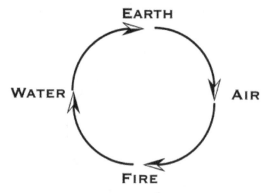

Elemental Transitions

Many also consider there to be a fifth element that transcends, but is also the foundation of the other four, and that is the element of Spirit.

Here are those elements and some of the common associations of each. Enter these into your BoW and add other qualities as you go. It is not important that you understand every association at this point. Each will become clearer as you begin to use them.

Item 7: The Elementals

Purpose: Preparation for ritual work. Preparation for magickal work. To develop an understanding of the natural forces that exist in life in relationship to four representative elements. To seek balance through an understanding of multiple forces.

Fire

Associations:	energy, strength, sex, protection, courage, anger, outer emotions, relationships
Items:	candle, hearth, wand, iron, red or orange stones, pike, matches, flint, ashes, torch
Magick:	candle, astral travel, sex magick

Water

Associations:	forms of uniting, psychic powers, dreams, alternative healing, inner emotions
Items:	cup, cauldron, bowl, pitcher, goblet, barrel, trident, cool liquid, wine cask, silver, blue stones, convex shield, seashells
Magick:	cleansing, healing

Air

Associations:	forms of dissipation, travel, intellectual pursuits, communication, philosophy, values
Items:	athame, feather, dagger, spear, wind instruments, letter opener, pen/pencil, fan, smoking pipe, copper, yellow stones, arrow
Magick:	visualization, divination

Earth

Associations:	matter, prosperity, traditional healing, grounding, business, finances, the physical
Items:	disk, wood, stones, clay, soil, salt, sand, herbs, bronze, green stones, knots
Magick:	grounding

Spirit

Associations:	centering, binding, essence
Items:	pentagram, candle, cords, binding objects, wheels, white or clear stones
Magick:	healing, energy work

As has already been mentioned, each of the four elements have many correspondences in nature and life. The following are some of these correspondences. These can be used in a variety of ways and there are many more that could be added.

Item 8. Properties and Correspondences Related to the Four Elements

Purpose: To relate different types of energies and forces that can be associated with the four elements. Can be used in designing ritual or magickal work.

	Air	Fire	Water	Earth	Spirit
Direction	East	South	West	North	Center
Color	yellow	red	blue	green	purple, black, clear
Tool	athame	wand	chalice	disk, censer	pentagram, pyramid
Instrument	air-blown	strings	bells	percussion	silence
Human Energy	mind	heart	soul	body	essence
Human Element	intellectual	emotional	spiritual	physical	true essence

Continued on next page.

	Air	Fire	Water	Earth	Spirit
Basic Needs	air	heat	water	food	love
Sense	smell	sight	taste	touch	sound
Temp.	warm	hot	cool	cold	none

Let's look at some of these correspondences in particular and see how they relate to each other. Many of these came from Celtic practices where the sea was mostly to the West and land and the mists stretched on to the East. This may make sense on the West Coast of the United States, but seems less logical to those on the East Coast. Be that as it may, most people still use the traditional four directions.

Air is related to the direction of East. East is where the sun first begins to rise and is the place for new beginnings. If East is where great stretches of land once were seen, then relating that direction to the element of Air would make sense because you could see across the land for great distances and could notice the oncoming winds. Yellow is associated with East to remind us of the color of the rising sun in the morning. The athame (pronounced a-tha-may), a ceremonial knife or sword, represents Air because of its ability to cut through space and to get at the truth. As a magickal tool, the athame can be used for the ceremonial cutting or marking of space. Some use the athame to draw a magick circle in ritual. In ritual, instruments into which air can be blown, such as woodwind or brass instruments, can be used to call this element. Air is the element of thought and mind. We seem to grasp our ideas "out of the air." This is also the element of travel and distance.

Fire is represented in the South where the sun is at its strongest and warmest. If you live in a warm climate, you know well the strength of the fire of the sun in summer. Fire often appears to us as red, and so red is the color of this element and direction. The wand is a tool used for directing energy. Fire is one of the most active forms of energy we know, and feeling heat in the body is often a good indication that energy has been raised. Therefore, the wand is a good tool for this element. Stringed instruments relate to the element of Fire especially when played hard and fast as in bluegrass music or in exciting classical pieces of music. The fire in our bodies is carried in our blood through the heart and that fire is expressed outwardly through our emotions. Many traditions relate the emotional side of the human spirit to water rather than fire. To me, water is calm and is related to the inner part of the human spirit. Fire is active and constantly changing, like our emotions. I relate the element of Fire to the outer emotions that we express to others—love, anger, distress, sorrow—these are emotions of high energy. Inner emotions, those things we feel and keep to ourselves, are the emotions I relate to the element of Water.

This brings us to **Water** itself. People living in the British Isles or along the shores of Northern and Western Europe would have seen great expanses of water to the West, and that is its traditional direction. When I began this book, the waters of Lake Champlain (New York) were to my west, and so I could relate to this same placement. Large bodies of water appear blue to us, so this has become the traditional color for West. The tool used in this direction is the chalice or cup that can hold water or other liquids. Instruments that resemble the chalice, such as bells, are good to use for this direction. As I have already mentioned, I relate the waters of West to deep inner and personal emotions and the sense of peace and calm that we all desire within. West is the direction of meditation and inner reflection. It is the home of the soul, which is, to me, the part of us that is most closely connected to the great mysterious Spirit of all things. The soul and Spirit are not the same things, but are intimately connected. A good analogy comes from the element of Water: The individual soul is like the drop of rain that returns to the ocean from which it came. Both raindrops and ocean are water, but the raindrop appears to be a separate entity. In reality, it is only a separate entity for a short time, but its essence remains that of the ocean. It is the same for the human soul that appears to be a separate entity from Spirit, but is not.

Earth is the element of the direction of North where the land spreads out in expanses of cold and snow. When I lived in Vermont, I experienced the awesome power of the earth through cold winds and powerful masses of ice and snow. The illusion that we are the dominators of nature is quickly swept away in the midst of a raging blizzard, and the strength and beauty of nature is revealed in the power of the trees that regularly withstand such beatings and flourish. For these reasons, the element of Earth can be represented in the colors of green or white, though green is the more traditional. The tool most associated with Earth is the disk—a flat, round plate. I some-times use a disk as a holder for my incense even though some put their incense in the East. I also usually put a special stone in North to represent Earth, which I call a dipping stone used to dip into blessed water to create a sacred space. Percussion instruments were once made from elements of the earth, such as tree trunks and animal skins, and represent well that element. That part of us that best relates to the element of Earth is our body, which is made of earthly materials (as well as a lot of water).

The fifth element, **Spirit,** resides in the center because it is the anchor of all the other elements. Without Spirit, all the other elements have no purpose and life would be meaningless. Purple represents spirituality and mystery and can represent Spirit, although black or, sometimes, clear can work as well. Spirit's tool varies with different traditions. Some place a pentagram in the center while others place representations of deities or other sacred objects. I use a pyramid, which, to me, is a three-dimensional representation of the five ele-ments that come together into one point. The four points of the base that rise to a single apex represent the coming together of the four elements into the unity of the fifth element—Spirit. In seeming oppo-sition to the other four elements whose instruments are all producers of great sound, the element of Spirit is represented by silence. This is not really an opposition, however, because all sound uses silence to create meaning. The part of Spirit related to the person is the true inner essence that makes us all part of the same reality.

The Phases of the Moon

Wicca is very much centered on the spirituality of nature. Wiccans celebrate the seasons of the sun, the changing phases of the moon, and the changing scene of the night sky created with the stars. It is a religion that practices real events that shape our lives. The changing position of the sun affects the seasons and our activities. The chang-ing phases of the moon affect other energies in our lives. The stars and planets also represent different energies such as those that make up our astrological sign.

The Goddess of Love is often symbolized by the moon. The changing face of the moon is perceived as a symbol of the many changing aspects of the Goddess. She is an Infant, a Maiden, a

Mother, and a Crone. Each phase of the moon affects the energies in our lives differently. Recent research indicates this idea may not be so far-fetched. When the moon is full, its energy is at its greatest. That energy is strong enough to affect the tides of the ocean (no small matter). Gardeners who are in tune with natural energies will tell you that it is best to plant when the moon is coming into its strength— waxing. If the moon's energies can affect all these things, then surely it must have other effects (however subtle) as well. As a practicing Wiccan, it is important to understand the phases of the moon and the energies associated with it.

With the changing faces of the moon, we celebrate the energies of the Goddess and her four aspects: Infant, Maiden, Mother, and Crone. The deity of the Child is celebrated when the moon is at its darkest and does not seem to be present.

Item 9. Phases of the Moon

Purpose: Identify the natural phases. To become more aware of these changes. To understand energies related to these changes for use in ritual or magickal work. To observe the changes these energies make in everyday life.

Dark of the Moon: A time for the celebration of the Child.

The dark of the moon is the time when the moon appears to be completely covered in darkness. This is the best time to view the great mystery of the stars and is the time for the celebration I call the Astor, or celebration, of the Child. This is a time for quietness and inner reflection and to appreciate the Great Mystery of life. Here, we can accept that we do not know all the answers and that those things we need to learn will be revealed in time. The dark of the moon is also a good time for scrying and other methods of divination.

New Moon: A time for the recognition of the Goddess in her phase as Infant.

The time of the new moon (the first two or three days the new crescent is visible) is a good time for celebrating new beginnings or doing magick which involves growth (starting a diet, beginning a new course of study, etc.). Here the first light in the cycle of the moon begins and the Goddess is in her phase as a young infant ready to explore the new world.

Waxing Moon: A time for the recognition of the Goddess in her phase as Maiden.

As the moon grows in light, the energies of growth come with her. The day of the full moon and the day or two just before the calendar day of the full moon are the best times for doing magick for bringing something to you (a new job, prosperity, good luck, etc.). During this time, we recognize the Goddess as the young Maiden who searches for a partner with whom she can become a new Mother. The Maiden is full of fresh energy and is anxious to sing and dance throughout the world.

Full Moon: A time for the recognition of the Goddess in her phase as Mother and a time to celebrate the Goddess.

The full moon is when the moon's energy is at its peak. The full moon is the best time for consecrating tools, charging jewelry, working magick to bring something to you, and for raising energy for the earth or other healing. It is also traditionally the time when Wiccans gather to celebrate the power of the moon through an esbat ceremony. It is during this time that the Goddess becomes the strong Mother figure who cares for the earth and all its creatures. This is truly a joyous time for celebration.

Waning Moon: A time for the recognition of the Goddess in her phase as Crone.

The waning moon, especially the days just before the dark of the moon, are best for doing magick for removing something from your life (bad habits, stress, etc.) or for clearing out negative energies. This is the time when the moon's energy is becoming weaker and the strength of the light of the Goddess is diminishing. This is a time of great wisdom, for she has learned much in her journey from Infant to wise Crone, and it is a time to learn from this wisdom by going within and communicating with her. This is a time of personal reflection and inner guidance. Soon the light of the Goddess will fade completely before the cycle will begin again.

Most Wiccans celebrate the full moon with a special ritual called the *esbat*. Some traditions even give each new moon a special name. Many different names are used and you should create your own to reflect common events related to your area. For example, if your community has an apple festival every September, you could call the full moon in September the Apple Moon. The following chart offers some additional examples.

Item 10. Names of the Full Moon

Purpose: For esbat celebrations.

Month	Moon Name	Description
January	Cold Moon	a time when temperatures are the coldest
February	Snow Moon	for many, this is a time of heavy snow
March	Sugar Moon	when maple syrup is harvested in the North
April	Wind Moon	the winds of early spring come howling
May	Flower Moon	the time of the first signs of spring
June	Long Days Moon	the summer days grow the longest
July	Honey Moon	honey is harvested and mead is made
August	Corn Moon	the time when corn is harvested
September	Harvest Moon	other vegetables are harvested and great feasts take place
October	Blood Moon	the time of the pre-winter slaughter
November	Remembrance Moon	a time for the remembrance of departed ones
December	Long Nights Moon	when winter nights grow the longest
Blue Moon		a mysterious and rare time of magick (second full moon in a month)

The Great Wheel

The phases of the moon also represent an even more powerful symbol: the Great Wheel. This diagram of the phases of the moon and their relationship to natural patterns contains a great deal of information. To understand it, we will assemble it a little at a time. We begin with the phases of the moon that we have already observed. Keep in mind that the phases do not actually relate to the moon itself but to the degree of light that it reflects back to the earth. Thus, the phases illustrate changes in degree between light and dark. This constant cycle of light changing to dark and then returning to light is a major theme in the Wiccan understanding of life and its cycles of change and renewal. If we put the four phases of the moon's changes in a circle, it is easy to see the cycle of change.

Item 11. The Great Wheel—
Representations of the Moon's Phases

Purpose: To observe the changing cycles of nature. To become more aware as an active participant in these cycles. To develop a calendar of cycles so that these may be celebrated and used.

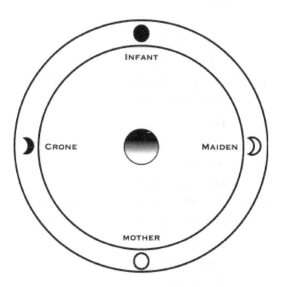

The Great Wheel and the Moon Phases

The top of the circle represents total darkness, while the bottom represents light. The moon is in a constant cycle of renewal from darkness to light and back to darkness. The four aspects of the Goddess: Infant, Mother, Maiden, and Crone also relate to the cycle of life. We each begin as a small child (the Infant), develop into a sexual being who seeks a mate (the Maiden or Suitor), become an adult who cares for others (the Mother or Father), grow into an older experienced teacher (the Crone or Sage), and then die—return to the darkness. It is this observation of nature that has taught Wiccans about the cycles of life and death, and it is for this reason that most Wiccans believe in some form of reincarnation. Just as the new moon is reborn into the full moon, so must life also return in some new form. The following is a chart of these phases of life as related to the phases of the moon.

Item 12. The Cycles of Life

Purpose: Can be used for personal or group rituals celebrating important passages in life. Can be used for designing Coming of Age ceremonies for others.

Age: 1–13
Moon phase: New (1st quarter)
Season: Late winter
Stage: Infant/Child
Characteristics: The young child sees the world as full of mystery and adventure.

Age: 14–27
Moon phase: Second quarter
Season: Spring
Stage: Maiden/Suitor
Characteristics: The Maiden comes to know herself and seeks to join in union with others and the special other.

Age: 28–41
Moon phase: Full (third quarter)
Season: Summer
Stage: Mother/Father

Characteristics:	The Mother accepts responsibility and offers care, love, and protection to others. (This doesn't necessarily have to mean your own children.)
Age:	42–55
Season:	Autumn
Stage:	Crone/Sage
Characteristics:	The Crone reflects back on a long life. This is the time to determine what legacy the person will leave to the world and a time to pass on wisdom and experience to others.
Age:	56-plus
Season:	Winter
Stage:	Ancient
Characteristics:	The Ancient returns to the spirit she had as a child. Free of responsibilities, she takes this final chance to live life fully while preparing for the next journey.

What is fascinating about the Great Wheel is that it can be related to many other natural cycles. Consider the phases of the sun. Though it does not change from light to dark, the spinning of the earth round the sun does create times of varying degrees of darkness and the four phases of the effects of the sun's energy on the planet that we call the four seasons. Winter is the darkest time of the year, while summer is the brightest. We can now put these phases onto the Great Wheel as well.

Item 13. The Great Wheel–

Representations of the Seasons

Purpose: To see the relationship of seasons to each other.

In the summer, the amount of daylight is at its highest degree. At the Spring Equinox, the light of day is equal to the light of night. During winter, darkness reigns over light, and at the Fall Equinox, the light and dark are once again balanced.

But the sun also affects the cycle of the days. At noon, the sun's light is at its height; while at midnight, there is no sunlight at all. During dawn and dusk, the light of the sun is balanced by the darkness of night.

The Great Wheel and the Seasons

Item 14. The Great Wheel—
Representations of the Times of the Day

Purpose: To observe relationships of the times of day to each other.

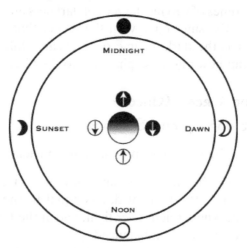

The Great Wheel and the Times of the Day

Wiccans celebrate the changes of the cycles of the sun just as they celebrate the phases of the moon. These celebrations are called *sabbats*, or sun ceremonies. There is a total of eight common sabbats. The four minor sabbats are related to the times when the seasons change and can be seen as appearing on the quarters of the Great Wheel. Yule (midwinter) is celebrated at the Winter Solstice, Ostara at the Spring Equinox, Litha (midsummer) at the Summer Solstice, and Mabon is celebrated at the Fall Equinox. Each of these four days of celebration are seen as the beginning of each season. Four other days are celebrated in between the beginnings of each season. It is on these days that the season and its related energy is considered to be at its height. Thus, these other four days appear on the cross-quarters of the Great Wheel and are considered to be the higher sabbats. These four are Imbolc (the height of winter), Beltane (the height of spring), Lughnasadh, or Lamas (the height of summer), and Samhain (the height of fall).

Item 15. The Great Wheel—
Representations of the Eight Sabbats

Purpose: To see the relationship of sabbats to each other.

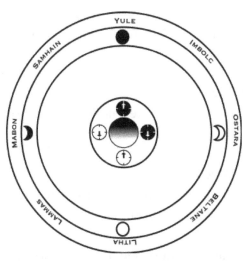

The Great Wheel and the Eight Sabbats

Item 16 details the eight sabbats and their related time of year. If you are to become a practicing Wiccan, you should observe each of the sabbats. Each are significant times of the year for all of life, but especially for those who worship the cycles of nature as a spiritual experience. In ancient times, the sabbats were important times for planting and harvesting crops. Each time of the year was related to specific duties that had to be carried out to meet the daily needs of the people. The waning of the sun's light was also seen to be the death of the God—the Goddess's child and consort. In the following lists, the dates of each sabbat are given along with the event in the story of the God and Goddess and an activity that can be used to help celebrate that particular sabbat. Colors that can be used in celebrations or seasonal representations are also included (the first color is the main color). For example, the cloth on the altar can be changed according to the main color of the season.

Item 16. The Sabbats

Purpose: To observe the traditional dates of the sabbats through ceremony or ritual.

Samhain

Date:	October 31
Season:	Height of fall, final preparations for winter, final harvest
Colors:	Black, white, orange
Celebration:	The God dies
Activity:	Remember those who have passed on

Yule

Date:	December 22
Season:	Winter Solstice, the sun's light returns
Colors:	White, red, green
Celebration:	The God is reborn
Activity:	Carve a sun symbol on a Yule log and burn it

Imbolc

Date:	February 1
Season:	Height of winter, look forward to the spring

Colors: Purple, white, yellow
Celebration: The God is consecrated and initiated
Activity: Light every candle in the house; also a good time for initiations

Ostara

Date: March 21
Season: Spring Equinox, the light and dark are equal
Colors: Yellow, green, blue
Celebration: The Goddess and the God court, the Goddess conceives
Activity: Take a celebratory walk in the country

Beltane

Date: May 1
Season: Height of spring
Colors: Green, yellow, red
Celebration: The God weds the Goddess
Activity: Join two things together in a ritual marriage

Litha

Date: June 21
Season: Summer Solstice, the sun's light is strongest
Colors: Red, yellow, blue
Celebration: The God is at the height of his power
Activity: Watch the sun rise

Lughnasadh (Lammas)

Date: August 1
Season: Height of summer, the sun's light is waning, first harvest
Colors: Brown, blue, red
Celebration: The God and Goddess celebrate their riches
Activity: Harvest and feast

Mabon

Date: September 21

Season: Fall Equinox, light and dark are equal, the second harvest

Colors: Blue, yellow, orange

Celebration: The God grows old and weak

Activity: Collect dried plants

The Cycles of the Sun

Just as we looked at the cycles of the moon from new to waxing and then from the new to the waning moon, we can look at the seasons of the sun in a similar way. It is true that the light of the sun does not actually change. Because of the elliptical shape of the earth, however, it appears and feels to us as if it does so. The sun shines its greatest amount of light at Litha and the least amount is seen at Yule. It feels to us, then, as if the sun is waxing between Yule and Litha and waning on the return back to Yule.

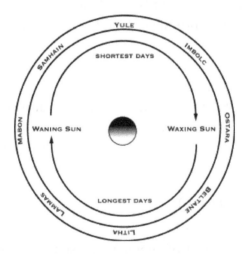

The Cycles of the Sun

If we view the seasons in this way, each season may appear to us as part of a greater sun cycle. In our celebration of the sabbats, we can use the same principle of waxing and waning as we do with the moon in order to give the sabbats additional meaning. When the sun is waxing, we can begin to manifest in our lives things that will bring light and joy into the lives of ourselves and others. During the waning sun, we can do the opposite and find ways of eliminating those things that bring sorrow. Consider adding the qualities in Item 17 to your sabbat rituals.

Item 17. The Cycles of the Sun

Purpose: To add greater depth to sabbats.

Waxing Sun

Imbolc: A time of initiations, to imagine what things you would like to bring to fruition, and to dream and consider plans for initiating those dreams.

Ostara: A time to determine and engage in concrete actions that will bring about your hopes and dreams for yourself and others, and to bring ideas to fruition.

Beltane: A deadline for your plans that you have set in motion, a time to assess your progress and to complete your goals.

Litha: A time for great celebration and mirth for having done good work.

Waning Sun

Lughnasadh: A time to determine what things need to be eliminated in order to reduce sorrow and suffering in your life and the lives of others.

Mabon: A time to determine an action in order to accomplish your goals, and to put into action that which will reduce suffering.

Samhain: A deadline for your plans that you have set in motion; a time to assess your progress, to complete your goals, and to commemorate the deeds of others.

Yule: A time of rest and reflection, and a time to store up energy for the coming seasons.

Magickal Alphabets

Wiccans today often enjoy writing their works using special alphabets or writing systems. Some use these alphabets as a way to make their work more secret to others or to make their writings available only to others who also know the same alphabet. There are a variety of known or created alphabets, but three have come into common use today. Though it may not be necessary to use these to hide secret work, it is still fun to work with them. Of course, you can feel free to make up a secret alphabet of your own—something only you can understand. That may also be the disadvantage, though. No one else will be able to read your work unless you provide a key, and if you lose that key, you might not be able to read your own writings. Jot down these three alphabets into your BoW and experiment with them. They can be used in a variety of ways and several of the scripts have special symbolic significance attached to each letter. These symbols will be studied later.

Runes

This series of 24 characters is based on vertical, diagonal, and crosshatch lines only. This simplicity makes the characters easy to learn and create. Another interesting advantage to this system is that letters can be combined in unique ways to create new symbols called *sigils*.

The word "rune" itself means secret or mystery, and the mystery is revealed when the meanings and interpretations of each symbol are understood. Runes were developed in Northern Europe. As to exactly when or where, many disagree, but it is fairly certain that the system or similar systems were in use by 200 B.C.E. The straight lines were created by carving lines into pieces of wood whose grain would have been placed horizontally. That is why there are no horizontal lines in the runes. In Norse mythology, the great god Odin, after a nine-day ordeal of self-torture, gave the runes to mankind to discover the secrets hidden in their mysterious shapes.

There are many variations of runes. Following is the set of runes most commonly used called the Elder Futhark (so named because the first six characters spell out F-U-Th-A-R-K) with the equivalent of each symbol to Arabic letters.

Item 18. The Runes

Purpose: Secret writings for inscribing names and words on tools, for use in written ritual and spellwork, to create rune sigils.

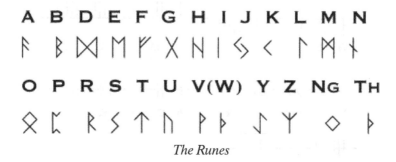

The Runes

The Ogham Alphabet

The ogham alphabet is also composed of a series of slashes based on a horizontal line. One advantage for using this system is that it barely appears to be an alphabet at all.

It is believed that the ogham alphabet originated with the Druids from at least as early as 200 B.C.E., though some have claimed earlier dates. These symbols may also have been carved into pieces of wood or they may have been created with long thin sticks. Another legend has it that Druid priests made the symbols with their fingers curved over their walking canes as secret signals to other priests. Just as with the runes, ogham symbols have divinatory meanings. Each symbol is related to a particular tree and the magickal significance associated with that tree.

Item 19. The Ogham Alphabet

Purpose: Secret writings for inscribing names and words on tools, for use in written ritual and spellwork.

Trees associated with each letter:

B = Birch	L = Rowan	F = Alder
S = Willow	N = Ash	H = Hawthorn
D = Oak	T = Holly	C = Hazel
Q = Apple	M = Vine	G = Ivy

NG = Broom   Z = Blackthorn   R = Elder
A = Fir   O = Gorse   U = Heather
E = Aspen   I = Yew

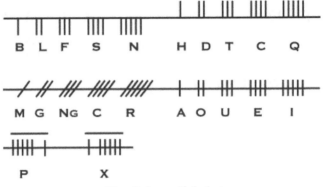

The Ogham Alphabet

The Theban Alphabet

Probably the most popular script with Wiccans for general writing is the ornate Theban alphabet. It may take a little longer to learn and master, but it makes for a very fancy text when used.

The origin of the Theban script is locked in mystery. It was probably created during the Renaissance when several different magickal traditions were being developed. Theban characters bear a close resemblance to certain alchemical alphabets of the 16th century and before. Some claim that a Renaissance magician named Honorius was the originator of the script, while others claim it was Dr. John Dee who developed the script and the tradition known as Enochian magick. Regardless of its history, the ornate Theban characters have become popular with Wiccans who enjoy working with a secret script.

Item 20. The Theban Alphabet

Purpose: Secret writings for inscribing names and words on tools, for use in written ritual and spellwork.

A	B	C	D	E	F	G	H	I	J	K	L	M
ꝰ	ꞁ	ꝏ	ꝯ	ꝑ	ꝓ	Ꞁ	ꝗ	U	ꝰ	ꝡ	ꝣ	ꝳ

N	O	P	Q	R	S	T	U	V	W	X	Y	Z	AND
ꝳ	ꝏ	ꝓ	ꝳ	ꝳ	ꝯ	ꝳ	X	ꞌ	ꝳ	ꝳ	ꝳ	ꝳ	ꝳ

The Theban Alphabet

Ethics

There are many who will tell you how they think you should act as a practitioner. But, as in everything else, it is important that you develop your own guidelines. With the understanding that these things may change as you study, take some time to formulate your own statement of belief. Wiccans believe that each person is capable of becoming a Priest or Priestess, and, indeed, you are currently in a process of study to becoming one.

A personal code of conduct is nothing more than a list of promises one makes to one's self as a guide for acting with others. This code of conduct must be based on personal beliefs and must be originated internally. An example of a code of conduct is the traditional code known as the Wiccan Rede. It contains the same principle of "As it harm none...," as well as the principle of the Threefold Law, which is the Wiccan understanding of balancing and returning energy. This is a principle similar to the law of Karma, which states any energy or intent sent into the universe will be returned. The Threefold Law goes a step further by claiming that any energy sent out is returned to the sender, but is strengthened by a power of three. Therefore, sending out negative energy or wishing to cause harm to another results in a return of that same type of energy magnified by three times the strength. The flip side of this idea is that good energy may also be amplified when returned. By understanding this law, then, it makes sense to do positive and loving work not only for the sake of others, but because equally positive energy will eventually be returned to you. Remember, however, that these things take place outside of the normal region of time and space in which we live our day-to-day lives and that there is no way of knowing how or when these energies will eventually manifest themselves.

Item 21. The Wiccan Rede

Purpose: An example of a code of conduct.

> *Bide the Wiccan Law Ye must*
> *In perfect love and in perfect trust.*
> *Nine words the Wiccan Rede fulfill*
> *An' as it harm none, do what Ye will.*
> *What Ye sends forth comes back to thee.*
> *So ever mind the Rule of Three.*
> *Thus, bright the cheek and warm the heart*
> *As Merry Ye Meet and Merry Ye Part.*

Symbolism of the Craft

As an esoteric religion, Wicca depends on the use and creation of a great deal of symbols. At this stage of learning, it is important to catalog these symbols and be able to recognize the basic shapes. Many of these symbols have a great deal of meaning and practice associated with them. Some involve systems of intense learning that will come later. For now, enter these symbols into your BoW. You may have seen many of these before and, if you continue to study, you will certainly see many of them again.

One of the most important symbols in Wicca is that of the five-pointed star known as the pentagram. Its five points represent the four elements (Air, Earth, Fire, and Water) plus the fifth element—Spirit. The fifth element is represented by the uppermost point so that the element of Spirit is seen as dominant over the other four. This is meant to represent that the spiritual life is the most important pursuit for the true practicing Wiccan. It does not deny that we need the other elements. We all need money and a place to live; we all need to be loved and honored; we all need the chance to be creative and thoughtful and to have those thoughts expressed without fear of retribution, but all these things must be gained in the light of spiritual understanding or else these things and life itself will feel meaningless and hollow.

The Pentagram

Item 22. The Pentagram

Purpose: Identification of meaning related to the primary symbol of Wicca.

SPIRIT

AIR   **WATER**

EARTH   **FIRE**

Spirit Over the Four Elements

The pentagram has some further symbolism as well. If you stand up, stretch out your arms to your side, and spread your feet about shoulder-width apart, you can take on the appearance of a five-pointed star. The pentagram, then, can also represent humanity. Wicca recognizes that all things are holy and contain the essence of the gods—this includes people. The five-pointed star reminds us that we are also sacred and that the gods depend on us to exist in this world. We worship the sacredness of all things because we are sacred as well. The number five is the number of the human body. Notice that we have five appendages (five fingers on each hand, five toes on each foot, and two arms, two legs, and a head, which equals five) as well as five senses.

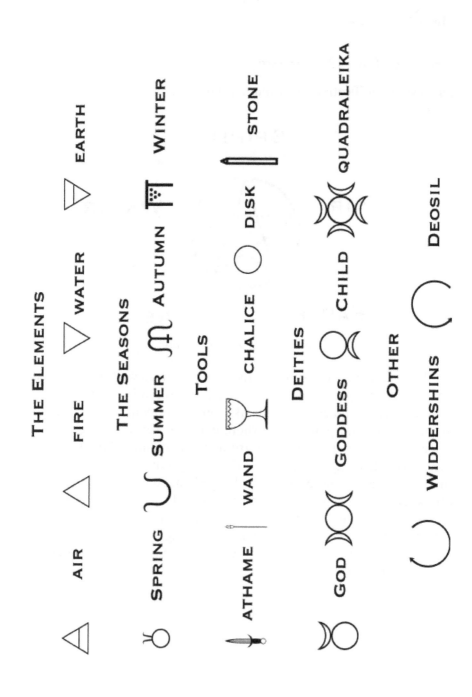

THE ELEMENTS

AIR   FIRE   WATER   EARTH

THE SEASONS

SPRING   SUMMER   AUTUMN   WINTER

TOOLS

ATHAME   WAND   CHALICE   DISK   STONE

DEITIES

GOD   GODDESS   CHILD   QUADRALEIKA

OTHER

WIDDERSHINS   DEOSIL

Finally, the pentagram also represents a star—another potent symbol. Stars are seen as small lights that pierce the darkness of night. A star reminds us that all is not lost; there is hope in the darkness. Stars are symbols of guidance. For centuries, sailors depended on the stars to guide them to their destinations. Stars also symbolize secret wisdom. By looking at the stars, ancient peoples saw entire stories, battles, and fables. These stories and star patterns were seen as messages from the gods given to people to discover for guidance. Even today, we interpret star patterns in the practice of astrology. The symbolism and meaning of this simple design, the five-pointed star, is deep. The pentagram has a long history, and the study of its past and meanings throughout time can be very fascinating in and of itself.

There are many other symbols that are commonly used in different practices. Some of these are listed here, many of which will be used later.

Other Symbols

Item 23. Other Symbols

Purpose: Additional symbols to recognize and use (see page 70).

Wiccan History

A Pagan Time Line

Currently, the history of modern Paganism is at the center of a great deal of controversy. Many Wiccans claim an ancient heritage dating back before pre-Christian times to an era when, as many believe, cultures worshipped a great goddess figure instead of the male god figure that currently dominates most well-known religions. There is certainly evidence available to suggest that religions with a matriarchal focus did indeed exist, but how widespread and uniform this practice was is not known. In reality, the practice of Wicca as we know it today is a fairly modern creation based on possible ancient sources. The beginning of what we call Modern Wicca started with the publication of Gerald Gardner's book *Witchcraft Today*. Though Gardner did make an attempt to incorporate some of what he learned as ancient practices into his own, we also know that he created many of the rituals and practices himself based on other sources available around him. These influences included the practices and writings of Aleister Crowley and other sources such as the book *Aradia* by Charles Leland. So, the practice we call Wicca today includes influences from Celtic practices, English mystics and temple worshipers, Italian sources, and a touch of plain old intuitive ingenuity. The following is a time line that shows early and modern influences on the development of the modern Pagan movement.

Item 24. A Pagan Time Line

Purpose: To observe the many possible sources of Wiccan historical development.

Possible Pre-Celtic Influences

B.C.E.

2500   Mystery cults develop in Minoa, Egypt, and other cultures.

2000   Greek civilization inherits mystery cults from the Minoans.

700   Romans absorb Greek and Etruscan practices.

600   Faery images appear in Etruscan art.

525   Pythagorus establishes mystery school in Southern Italy.

400   Celts invade Northern Italy.

322   Alexander the Great conquers Egypt.

155   Critolaus formally introduces Greek philosophy in Rome.

50   Romans carry mystery teachings into Gaul.

30   Rome conquers Egypt.

C.E.

43   Romans carry mystery teachings into Britain.

150   Celts conquered by the Romans, who spread mystery teachings to the Celt farmers.

410   Romans withdraw from Britain.
       Romanticized Celtic religion spread throughout Britain.

600   First written mystery texts, including Taliesin.

Early Pagan Sources

1533   Henry Cornelius Agrippa's *Three Books of Occult Philosophy.*

     ◆   Detailed methods of magic.

1600   First modern (dedicated to ritual) Masonic lodges in Scotland.

1692   The "Burning Times."

1736   Witchcraft Act enacted in England.

     ◆   Ascribed punishments to those claiming to work magic.

1824   Vagrancy Act enacted in England.

     ◆   Outlawed any acts of divination or similar.

1866   *The Key of the Mysteries* and *Transcendental Magic* by Eliphas Lévi.

     ◆   English translations of earlier (1860) works written in French.

     ◆   Used the term "occult" to mean secret knowledge.

     ◆   Used pentagram as symbol of microcosm and hexagram (six-pointed star) as macrocosm.

     ◆   Use of four elementals.

     ◆   Use of invoking and banishing pentagrams.

1875   H.P. Blavatsky founds Theosophical Society in New York.

1877   *Isis Unveiled* by H.P. Blavatsky.

     ◆   Brings together concepts of Eastern and Western mysticism.

     ◆   Claims that all religions have some elements of the whole truth.

1881   *The Occult World* by A.P. Sinnet.

1884   Founding of the Hermetic Society.

     ◆   Advocated use of temples rather than lodges.

     ◆   Use of the four quarters related to directions and watchtowers.

     ◆   Use of working tools: chalice, sword, scourge.

1888   *The Secret Doctrine* by H.P. Blavatsky.
  ◆   Hermetic Order of the Golden Dawn founded.
1897   *Aradia* by Charles Godfrey Leland.
  ◆   Advocates the celebration of Diana on the full moon.
  ◆   Use of cakes and ale.
1903   *Prolegomena to the Study of Greek Religion* by Jane Ellen Harrison.
  ◆   Related mother, maiden, and an unnamed third to moon phases.
1904   *Book of the Law* by Aleister Crowley.
1921   *The Witch Cult in Western Europe* by Margaret Murray.
  ◆   Stated theory of ancient goddess traditions.
  ◆   Covens of 13 people.
  ◆   Celebrations of four sabbats.
1922   *The Golden Bough* (abridged and updated version) by Sir James Frazer.
  ◆   Proposed ancient belief in a dying god related to cycles of vegetation.
1929   *Magick in Theory and Practice* by Aleister Crowley.
  ◆   Inverted pentagram as matter over spirit.
  ◆   Used tools: oil, bell, censer, book of spells.
  ◆   Introduced the word "magick" to distinguish from sleight of hand.
1947   Gerald Gardner (1884–1964) and Aleister Crowley (1875–1947) meet.

Modern Wicca

1947   It is commonly believed that Gardner and Dafo start the New Forest Coven, England.
1948   *The White Goddess* by Robert Graves.
  ◆   Discussed the triple goddess with the word "crone."
  ◆   Claimed that ancient goddess religions were deeply encoded in ancient poetic sources.

1949 *High Magic's Aid* by Gerald Gardner.

 ◆ Use of athame.

 ◆ Introduced Gardner's Book of Shadows.

 ◆ Made women an equal part of ceremonies.

 ◆ Celebrated eight sabbats.

1951 Repeal of English Witchcraft and vagrancy laws.

1954 *Witchcraft Today* by Gerald Gardner.

1965 Alexander Sanders's first coven publishes its Book of Shadows.

 ◆ Coven emphasizes more high magick in ritual.

1966 "Regency" coven founded by followers of Robert Cochrane.

 ◆ Use of black robes.

 ◆ Eliminated the scourge.

 ◆ Preferred outdoor rituals.

 ◆ Elements: Air = West, South = Fire, West = Water, North = Earth.

1971 *What Witches Do* by Stewart Farrar.

 ◆ Comprehensive discussion and rituals of Gardnerian tradition.

1975 *An ABC of Witchcraft Past and Present* and *Natural Magic* by Doreen Valiente.

 ◆ Made self-initiation possible.

 ◆ Emphasized correspondence with nature.

 ◆ Magick could be used for good by anyone.

 ◆ Created original charges of the gods.

1979 *Spiral Dance* by Starhawk.

 ◆ Related magick in terms of psychology.

 ◆ Energy is the essence of magick.

 ◆ Principles of Karma applied to magick.

 ◆ The gods are real forces from human energies.

Drawing Down the Moon by Margot Adler.

 ◆ Discussed Pagan history, but with an eye toward Wicca as a modern development.

1980   *The Holy Book of Women's Mysteries* by Z Budapest.
- Advocated strong feminist viewpoint to Witchcraft.

1988   *Wicca: A Guide for the Solitary Practitioner* by Scott Cunningham.
- Brought Doreen Valiente's approach to solitary Witchcraft to the United States.

Traditions

Once you have fully come to understand your own spiritual practice, it is equally important to take some time to understand the religious practices and traditions of others. Take some time to learn about the other main world religions. Read their texts and ponder their philosophies. Also, you should learn about other Pagan traditions and pantheons.

A Sample Pantheon: The Celtic Gods

Because many Wiccans associate their practice with European roots, some have come to adopt the ancient Celtic gods and goddesses as their deities of worship. There are a wide variety of traditions with gods and goddesses to choose from, but Celtic seems to remain the most popular. If you feel you need or desire the powerful energies of these ancient forces for positive growth and practice, then, by all means, do so, but try not to get caught up in serving just for the sake of being subservient or using the name of a god to avoid taking responsibility for your actions.

Item 25 provides a list of the Celtic deities known as the Tuatha De Danann (the people of the Goddess Danu). In ancient Celtic texts, the names of several different groups of invaders are mentioned. The Tuatha De Danann were one of those conquering invaders, but the stories of their victories mythologized the lives of those heroes until they began to take on god-like status. They were human, but divine humans. By the time they were eventually conquered, a pantheon of gods had developed from the stories of these heroes. It is said that the Tuatha De Danann were not actually destroyed. Instead, they fled into the many mounds in the countryside and became the mystical faery folk that are so popular in Irish legends.

Item 25. The Celtic Gods

Purpose: For use in ritual or magickal work.

Aine:	Goddess of the Western ocean; sky goddess.
Aonghus:	God of love and youth.
Badb:	Goddess of war; part of the Triple Goddess.
Banbha, Fodhla, Eriu:	Goddess of sovereignty.
Boand:	The consort of Dagda; goddess of the river.
Brigit:	Goddess of culture and poetry, and daughter of Dagda.
Cernunnos:	The "Horned God." God of nature, virility, fertility, animals, sex, reincarnation, and shamanism.
Dagda:	The All Father; many talented and powerful. Lord of great knowledge.
Danu:	Mother Goddess. The daughter of Dagda and earth goddess of plenty.
Ler:	The god of the sea.
Lugh:	Sun god and a hero god. He is master of all arts, skills, and crafts.
Macha:	The third of the triad of goddesses known as the Morrighan; fertility goddess.
Medb:	The drunken woman. A goddess of war.
Morrighan:	The dark aspect of the Celtic Triple Goddess.
Nuadhu:	The King and battle leader.
Ogma:	The god of wisdom, eloquence, and language.

After studying the Celtic pantheon, consider studying an additional different pantheon. There are many to choose from, and all offer unique perspectives. Pantheons can be studied from popular cultures such as Egyptian, Mesopotamian, Greek, Roman, Welsh, Scandinavian or Norse, African, and the cultures of the Pacific Islands such as Hawaii, Aztec, Mayan, Native American, Chinese, and Japanese, just to name a few.

The Basics of Ritual

The Altar

One of the most important aspects of this religion is the development of a personal altar, and to learn how to use that altar in personal rituals. First, it is important to understand the purpose of ritual.

Strictly speaking, a ritual is anything done routinely and habitually, but this is not the type of ritual we are discussing here. We are concerned with sacred ritual. This is an act to which a spiritual meaning is ascribed. Eating dinner is a ritual, especially if it is done in a similar manner and at the same time each evening. Eating dinner is not a sacred ritual unless you attach special meaning to what you are doing. The Christian Eucharist is a sacred ritual because the food and drink consumed is given special meaning by those taking part. The same is true of a Wiccan ritual. Simply putting things on a table and lighting candles is not a sacred ritual unless special meaning is attached to those actions.

The purpose of a spiritual ritual practice is to separate the practitioner from the mundane activities of everyday life. During a ritual, the repeated actions have the effect of slowing down time—moving away from the fast-paced activities that are so common to normal life. By putting on a robe, lighting special incense, speaking special words, and using unique symbols as well as all the other parts of a traditional Wiccan ritual, the practitioner creates a unique space and sets aside daily worries.

Most Wiccan rituals reflect the spiritual understanding of the practitioner. We have already discussed the five elements and some symbolism. Now we will see how they can be used to create a sacred altar. Most Wiccan altars reflect the use of four elements (Earth, Air, Fire, Water) by assigning each one of the elements a direction, a working tool (or set of tools), and a color. Refer back to the properties of the elements (page 48) to see the traditional assignment of each of these. The altar also has representations of the deities and an object in the center that represents the fifth element—Spirit. In the following sample altar, the four directions are used to represent the four main elements. Each direction has one or two working tools and a candle in the represented elemental color. In the center is the pentagram as a representation of Spirit. Four candles are used. The three uppermost are to represent the God, the Goddess, and the Child. The candle in the South, called the working candle, is a small candle used to represent your stated intent and for lighting all other candles.

Item 26. The Ritual Altar

Purpose: An example for creating a personal altar space. (See page 70 for symbol meanings.)

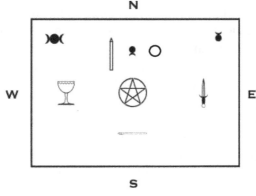

Ritual Altar

Ritual Tools

The diagram of the ritual altar shows several different tools placed in each of the four directions. Again, use whatever tools you feel are necessary for your own practice and place them wherever you need. Review the previous information about the four directions and their correspondences to get a feel as to where your own tools should go.

The athame is a small knife or sword used in ritual work. Most suggest that it be a double-edged blade and that it not be used to cut any material. It is used to cut or mark magickal space such as the circle around your altar. Because it is used to cut through the air to create a sacred space, the athame is usually considered a tool of the element of Air and it is placed in the East. Some traditions (including the one in which I began my training) put the athame in the South because swords are forged in fire and so represent that element. Other tools that can be placed in the East are ceremonial bells and the candle snuffer.

The working candle is placed in the South. The flame of the candle represents the element of Fire and the active principle. Fire is the element of energy, and lighting the working candle is a part of the ritual in which you make clear your intention. In a practical sense, if the working candle is to be the first one lit and the last candle extinguished, then it is good to have that candle near to you as you work. Another common tool of Fire is the wand. Because it is often wielded in the air similar to the athame, some place the wand in the East. The wand is an instrument of directed energy. When you have the need to direct your energy toward an object or toward a location, the wand can be a helpful tool to use. For me, because it is an instrument used to direct energy, the wand is a tool of the element of Fire—the symbol of active energy.

The use of the chalice in the West was discussed on page 50. Because a cup is an instrument for holding liquid, it makes sense to have the chalice in the direction of the element of Water. A vial of water that you may have blessed is also often placed in the West. Some also add a cauldron or small pot in the West, which can be used for burning objects or for mixing liquids and herbs.

North is the direction for the element of Earth. So, it makes sense to put herbs or stones in this location. Some use salt as a purifying agent in their work. Although it is very traditional to do so, I use salt very rarely. The reason being that throwing salt around inside can damage floors and carpets and using salt outside can be detrimental to some plants. I use what I call a dipping stone, which is a long shaped stone or crystal (usually green to represent Earth) that is dipped into the chalice of water. Depending on where you are working, splashing water around may not be beneficial to the furniture, but I have found it to be less damaging and easier to clean up than salt or herbs.

I also place my incense burner (disk) and incense in the North. The traditional placement of the incense is in the East because the smoke of the incense represents the element of Air. However, my incense burners are usually in the shape of a small disk, which is the symbol for the element of Earth, and because the incense I burn is made from plants and minerals of the earth, I prefer to place my incense in the North. Practically speaking, I also prefer my incense to be on the far side of my altar so that I do not become overwhelmed by the smoke. Remember, practicality is an equally important factor to any ritual work.

Finally, a tool or object that represents Spirit should be placed in the center. Many use a pentagram to represent the five elements and the Craft itself. I use a pyramid, which, to me, represents the five elements (the pyramid has five sides if you include the base). The rising of four sides into one point represents the single source of the four elements.

As you can see, not all traditions or practitioners agree on the use, selection, or placement of tools for the altar. Decisions about these items must be based on thought, feeling, and also practicality. Item 27 provides is a listing of tools and placements discussed here.

Item 27. Ritual Tools

Purpose: An example of traditional Wiccan tools and their uses.

North (Earth)

Mineral or Herb
>Description: Purifying mineral or herb such as salt.
>Use: Purification and blessing.

Censer and Incense
>Description: Flat object used to hold and burn incense.
>Use: Purification and creating ritual space.

Dipping Stone
>Description: A white or green pointed stone.
>Use: To dip into the chalice water and spread around in a sacred circle for purification.

East (Air)

Athame
>Description: Double-edged ceremonial knife.
>Use: Casting circles, cutting doors, directing energy.

Bell

Description: Ringing bell.

Use: Purification, consecration, confirmation of events.

Snuffer

Description: Small cup-shaped object with handle.

Use: Snuff out candles.

South (Fire)

Wand

Description: Straight object with crystal at top.

Use: Directing energy, consecration, grounding.

Working Candle

Description: Small candle.

Use: For stating and consecrating intention, to light space for working.

West (Water)

Chalice

Description: Cup or bowl.

Use: Holding blessed water or wine for purification and consecration.

Blessed Water

Description: Consecrated water.

Use: To be poured into the chalice or sprinkled during purification.

Cauldron

Description: Large open container.

Use: For burning objects, collecting ashes and items to throw away, mixing things.

Center (Spirit)

Pentagram

Description: Five-pointed star in circle.

Use: Marking center, grounding all other objects, focus of concentration.

Pyramid

Description: A four-sided object with a base at the bottom and point at the top.

Use: To symbolize the joining of the four elements.

Ritual Procedure

Now that you have an idea of how to create an altar and know what the basic purpose of each tool is, you may want to consider performing your first full ritual. As with anything else, you are free to design your ritual in any manner you choose. I will offer you one way to do a ritual so that you may have a base from which to create your own.

Item 28. Ritual Procedure

Purpose: An example for creating a personal ritual procedure with sample chants.

1. Preparation.
    a. Assemble materials and make sure there will be no disturbances.
    b. Prepare the altar (see ritual circle).
        * Check for incense, moon water, lighter, salt or herbs, and candles.
    c. Prepare participants (bath, clothing, etc.).
2. State intention.
    a. Light working candle.

    It is I, [state common or magickal name], *who comes before thee to initiate this circle of power for the purpose I state*: [state specific purpose of ritual].
3. Banish and purify.
    a. Banish old energy, if necessary (ring bell at each corner), widdershins.

    If any ill intent here be, by these sounds I banish thee.
    b. Place athame in fire, draw invoking pentagrams at quarters, deosil.

By Air and Fire, purify.

   c. Place water in chalice. Put dipping stone and draw circle, deosil.

     By Water and Earth, purify.

   d. Light incense.

4. Cast the circle.

   a. Ground, center, and raise magickal energy.

     In this circle now I spin, a sacred rite shall soon begin.

     May I now be safe and sure for the work I here procure.

   b. Set marker(s) in circle and/or announce circle.

   c. Beginning from the East and continuing clockwise, set the four quadrants.

     ♦ Place ritual objects or light candles.

     Powers of the East, realm of the intellect, element of Air,
     I conjure thee—that there remain within this frame
     no adverse thought nor enmity. Hail and Welcome!
     Blessed be!

     Powers of the South, realm of emotions, element of Fire,
     I conjure thee—that there remain within this frame
     no adverse thought nor enmity. Hail and Welcome!
     Blessed be!

     Powers of the West, realm of the soul, element of Water,
     I conjure thee—that there remain within this frame
     no adverse thought nor enmity. Hail and Welcome!
     Blessed be!

     Powers of the North, realm of the body, element of Earth,
     I conjure thee—that there remain within this frame
     no adverse thought nor enmity. Hail and Welcome!
     Blessed be!

   d. Call the three deities (God, Goddess, Child).

     ♦ Place ritual objects or light candles.

     O Goddess of the Moon, great feminine one,
     bless this sacred circle and all work within it done.

O God of the Sun, great masculine one,
bless this sacred circle and all work within it done.

O Child of the Stars, great mysterious one,
bless this sacred circle and all work within it done.

   e.   Call the two layers (sky, earth).

O Father Sky above and Mother Earth below,
I stand in reflection to ask for your protection.

   f.   Place ritual pendant on self.

   g.   Bow to altar, announce circle is closed, ring bell.

And now at last, the circle is cast.

5.   Ritual.

   a.   Begin meditation and visualization on objective.

   b.   Begin specific magickal work or ritual.

6.   Completion.

   a.   Release layers in reverse order.

O Mother Earth below and Father Sky above,

I stand in reflection and thank you for your protection.

   b.   Release deities in reverse order.

O Child of the Stars, great mysterious one,
if you have come to bless this rite,
we thank you now for your bright light.

O God of the Sun, great masculine one,
if you have come to bless this rite,
we thank you now for your bright light.

O Goddess of the Moon, great feminine one,
if you have come to bless this rite,
we thank you now for your bright light.

   c.   Release quadrants in reverse order.

Powers of the West, depart. To your realm your light impart.
And if intent and will are true, to this work you shall ensue.
Powers of the South, depart. To your realm your light impart.
And if intent and will are true, to this work you shall ensue.

Powers of the East, depart. To your realm your light impart.
And if intent and will are true, to this work you shall ensue.

Powers of the North, depart. To your realm your light impart.
And if intent and will are true, to this work you shall ensue.

    d. Open the circle, ring bell.

Now this circle I undo for this sacred rite is through.
Let these blessings I bestow like a seed, take root and grow.
For the good of one and all, Blessed Be!

7. Ground yourself.

As above, so below.

Let's take a look at each of these steps in detail. Remember to use and change each practice as you need to make the ritual feel like your own.

The first step is to prepare the area and the participants (that's you unless you are going to have others join you). Make sure you have all the materials you need on your altar or that they are easily within your reach. Things such as incense and lighters are easy to forget, and once you create a circle of power around yourself, it is best not to leave your circle—not to mention, of course, that running out to the kitchen to look for matches can ruin the whole mood you spent so much time to create. Some people also take a special ritual bath or do other personal actions of cleansing or renewal before beginning. Others also put on special clothing such as robes and cloaks (while others work in the nude—skyclad). Of course, you could always just put on the sacred blue jeans.

Once your altar is set and prepared and you have done what you need to do to feel ready to begin, it is time to begin work on the altar itself. Either internally or externally, state your intention to the gods. In other words, clearly set out what you intend to do during this ritual and for what purpose. If you are not crystal clear on your own purpose, then nothing you do will be effective. You must have a vision in your mind of exactly what it is you wish to accomplish, celebrate, or honor with this ritual in order for that purpose to become manifest. After stating your purpose, light your working candle. Use a white candle for now because this is a standard color for basic ritual work (other colors and purposes will be discussed later).

In the next few steps, you will work directly with energy—the life force that flows within you and all things. When you are doing a ritual, you must first clear out any preexisting energy in your space so that nothing will interfere with your purpose. Then, you will begin to focus upon your own energy. You can feel this energy rising within you. Some feel it as heat or as a feeling of excitement and joy, while others see it through visualization. Each person will experience it differently, but it can be experienced. By focusing and directing this energy, great things can happen.

Banishing and purifying helps to establish in the mind of the practitioner that the space is being symbolically prepared for ritual work. By using the athame and drawing invoking pentagrams in the space, you are calling upon the elements of Fire and Air. By dipping a stone in a chalice of blessed water and spreading that water in a circle around you, you are calling upon the elements of Water and Earth. While doing these acts of purification, feel and/or visualize the clearing of remaining energies in the area. Finally, light incense and let the scent fill the room. This will literally "clear the air."

Now it is time to actually draw a circle around you. By creating this barrier between you and the ordinary world, you are clearing out a special place of power that can be beyond space, time, and all your daily concerns. This is a place for you to make direct contact with the gods in whatever way you see fit. We will discuss the concept of raising energy much later but, for now, simply quiet yourself in front of your altar and imagine that you draw up energy from the earth. Using your wand or another tool, stones or markers, or even just your finger, draw a circle around yourself. Make sure it is large enough to include your altar and to allow you enough room in which to work. Next, call upon or recognize each quarter starting from the East and moving clockwise. Then, if you so choose, call to your deities and recognize their presence and help. Using the working candle, light the candles in each of the four quadrants as you go and light the candles that represent the deities as you call to them. Some traditions also call to the layers of above and below to remind them that the circle they are creating also extends upward and downward, creating a complete three-dimensional sphere. Finally, place a pendant on yourself that announces that you are now engaged in ritual, bow to the altar and proclaim that the circle is closed. You are ready to get to work.

The next phase depends on the particular work or celebration you are engaged in. When you are done with this work, be sure to reopen the circle by going in the exact opposite order in which you created it. Release the two layers, the deities, the four quarters, snuff out the candles, and then open the circle in a counterclockwise direction. Release the energy you raised toward your goal. Again, feel or visualize this energy moving toward your goal to manifest good work. Your ritual is complete.

At the conclusion of your ritual, you should ground yourself. Wiccans believe that, with each ritual, excess energy may be raised. If this excess energy remains, it may cause sleeplessness or simple discomfort such as headaches. Simply stretch out on the ground and concentrate on allowing any remaining energy to return to the earth. Feel or visualize this energy draining from your body and returning to the earth. Stay grounded for as long as you feel necessary. When you are finished, you should feel relaxed and refreshed.

Item 29. An Invoking Pentagram

Purpose: For marking sacred spaces.

START HERE

Creating a Pentagram

Begin making an invoking pentagram by starting at the top and moving down to the right. Continue until the pentagram is complete. Notice that by going in this manner, the points of the pentagram are created in a clockwise fashion—suitable for invoking.

Perform Your First Ritual

Now the time has come for you to write and perform your first full ritual. Perform a basic ceremony to consecrate your altar and tools. Based on what you have learned so far, create a ritual circle and enact your altar. Then, consecrate your altar and all the tools you have obtained. Do not worry about whether you are doing it correctly. Let your mind guide you in the formalities and let your heart guide you to do the rest and it will be right. Remember, it is your intent that is most important in any ritual. You could do separate rituals to bless each of your tools that you obtain, or you could gather everything together and consecrate your altar and all your tools at once.

Item 30 is a sample of a ritual I often use to consecrate my altar. I do this ritual between sabbats when I change the color of the altar cloth to the new color of the season or when I need to set up the altar after taking it down. This ritual reflects my eclectic use of ideas from many different traditions and is an example of how different ideas can be used to create a very personal ritual. In it, I ritually bless and consecrate the entire altar and all the tools upon it. Design your own ritual for this purpose and be sure to write in your BoW what worked and what did not so that you can improve upon each ritual performed. Refer to the ritual procedure on pages 83–86.

Item 30. A Ritual of Consecration

Purpose: An example of a ritual used to consecrate a magickal altar and tools.

1. Clear altar space and clean area thoroughly.
2. Spread altar cloth and say the following:

   Sacred altar, realm of visions, symbol of the integrated being; the ground beneath my feet, accept and support the weight of my intent. Prepare the way for good works and offerings. For the good of one and all, so mote it be.

3. Set center object and say the following:

   Blessed catalyst of the center, representative of the mysterious void, anchor this altar for all other things placed here. O entity of center, element of universal self, blessed be.

4. Set altar objects from center out, clockwise starting with East. With each repeat:

    O entity and tool of [direction]*, element of* [element]*, blessed be.*

5. State intention.

    It is I, [state common or magickal name]*, who comes before thee to initiate this circle of power for the purpose I state: O great ones, I come before thee tonight to consecrate this altar and these tools. Bless and guide me in this work.*

6. Banish and purify the space.

7. Cast the circle.

8. Ritual: Meditate for a few moments and concentrate on the altar. Announce that the altar is hereby consecrated. Ring bell.

    O powers that here congregate, to righteous work these things I dedicate. To each my will and purpose integrate. This sacred altar and these tools I hereby consecrate.

9. Completion: Release layers, deities, and quadrants, and open the circle.

10. Ground yourself.

You may want to develop a daily ritual practice. Many people develop an early morning or late evening practice that helps to create a sense of balance between the mundane and the sacred parts of the day. Try to incorporate a small amount of ritual and meditation into each day, if possible. Even doing something just once a week can be beneficial. A tool to help you remember to both do your daily ritual and evening journal writing is a pendant that you wear around your neck during the day. In the morning, put your pendant around your neck and let it hang outside your clothing. This is to remind you to do your morning ritual. When you have done the ritual, slip the pendant under your shirt and let it remain there the rest of the day. The feeling of the pendant against your body will remind you of your commitment to the Craft. Before you go to bed at night, do not remove your pendant until you have written in your journal and done any nighttime ritual. This is just one possible method of practice. Enter the methods that you develop and any related notes into your BoW.

The Basics of Spellcraft

What Is Magick?

My definition of magick is "conscious transformation through will." When any two things are combined together to create something new that is greater than its parts, that is transformation. For example, the merging of hydrogen gas with oxygen can create water—something different and unique from its separate parts. Magic (without a "k") is transformation through illusion, while magick (with a "k") is real transformation. If that transformation is undirected, we call it luck or chance, but if that transformation is consciously directed, it is called creativity, which is the same thing as magick. (If you believe that the whole universe is directed by consciousness, however, then there would be no such thing as luck.) Transformations can only occur within the laws of physics. For example, the total energy of the universe must remain constant. Therefore, transformation must always involve certain amounts of existing energy to create something with an equal amount of energy. Much can happen within those bounds of physics, however.

Though magick touches everything, we are concerned here with the type of magick directed by ourselves. The most difficult type of magick to enact is that which transforms things other than ourselves, while the easiest type of magick is the kind that transforms ourselves. It is much easier to transform yourself into the type of person who can attract what you want rather than trying to force those things or people to you. Transform the way you think and act in the world and you will change the world around you. The true Wiccan does little spellwork because she has transformed herself into a joyous being who no longer needs so many things and people for her happiness. When an actual need is encountered, she concentrates on being the type of person who can attract that need to her. She may enact her spell, but she will be patient with the results and will believe completely in her heart that what she needs is truly necessary and that it will, without a doubt, come her way in time. This type of person understands the true workings of magick.

Magick is not the ability to fulfill whatever wish is desired. This is what most beginning Wiccans want, but one simply cannot light a few candles, say a few rhymed words, draw fancy symbols, and then receive whatever one's heart desires. As much as you may wish, I'm sorry to tell you that you cannot have whatever you want, whenever you want it! The laws of physics do not allow it. This does not mean you should not ask for the things you need. By all means, if you are in need of something, light a candle, speak your chant, and send out your desire to the gods, but keep in mind that it is the universe that will decide whether your wish will be granted.

Principles of Spellcraft

For Wiccans, the act of making a request to the gods or the universe is done through the casting of a spell. In spellwork, we are asking the universe to fulfill a need, but we believe that we are an equal part of making the needed result happen. We infuse our own energy with the energy of the universe toward a directed end. Spellcasting is an integral part of the tradition of Wicca, but it is also one of the most difficult and controversial aspects. There are many who say that magick and spellcasting are not really a true part of the Wiccan religion, while others say it is an integral part of the study. If magick and spellcasting are used as tools for spiritual development, then they can be a worthwhile part of your study.

It is important that you take time in carefully learning the principles and ethics of spellcasting before beginning. Understanding the principles of spells can take years of intense study, and a true understanding comes from a formulation of one's own vision of how the cosmos works—this is truly a spiritual understanding and not something to be taken lightly. If you have started this practice because you desire to cast spells that will supposedly allow you to control or influence others for personal gain, then you are in the wrong practice. This path is a spiritual path and all spiritual paths lead to a union with the Divine—a development that must dissolve the personal ego and its material desires.

To begin to practice magick, it is important to understand how it works. To engage in magick, spellcasting, divination, and healing, it is necessary to understand that the individual person is incapable of accomplishing anything alone. Each practitioner must connect to the gods through the unity of the one essence that is part of us all. It is through this energy of unity that all things are possible. But it is the connection to this source that is the most difficult process. The work must be done through all four elements by working with each of the four parts of our total being. These four parts are the mental, emotional, spiritual, and physical realms of the self. In our day-to-day life, we exist mostly on the material plane and our senses constantly reinforce our experience on this plane. But there are other more subtle planes of existence. It is through these planes that metaphysical phenomena occur. Wiccans believe in the reality of these phenomena. In fact, most people have had experiences of psychic occurrences in their lives but they are afraid to talk about it. These occurrences are common because of the reality of these other planes. Beyond the material plane is the plane of the elements. We have already discussed some of the qualities of the elements. It is believed that all things that exist are formed with the essence or the qualities of one of the four elements. It is also here that the four realms of the self exist so that they can be coordinated together on the material plane. Beyond the elemental plane is the plane of the gods—the energies of complimentary opposites that give all things life—and just beyond that plane is the plane of the one true essence.

Item 31. Planes of Existence

Purpose: To understand the way of connecting to the inner essence.

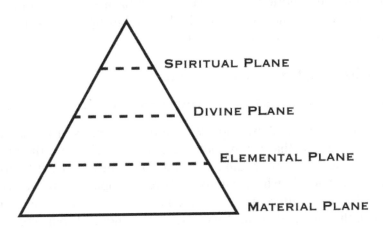

Planes of Existence

Beyond the physical planes are higher energies of each part of the self. Beyond the physical body is the auric body. This is an energy body that does not have a physical reality as the physical body does. It can never be tested or examined through medical means because experimentation of this sort is purely physical. It can, however, be experienced through nonphysical experiences. We will take a look at how each element can be accessed.

Western psychology has already experienced the second level of the mental realm—that of the unconscious. It is already quite well understood that the unconscious is a nonphysical, deeper aspect of the mental self, and it was Carl Jung who introduced the concept of the next mental level—the collective unconscious. What is little understood is that the same is true for all the other parts of the self. For the emotional part of the human self, deeper levels are attained by reaching to the highest level of the purest emotion—true unconditional love. To understand love from the viewpoint of the unattached self—the kind of love that gives without asking in return, that forgives without condition or reservation—is to relate to the highest level of the emotional self, for that kind of love is the energy that binds the universe.

The spiritual side of the self also has a higher level, but to experience it, one must go beyond the self to a point of selflessness—to the point where you no longer experience yourself as an individual being, but as a part of an indivisible whole. By reaching these deeper levels of the mental, emotional, spiritual, and physical self, you can access greater energies and work magick. The following chart in Item 32 illustrates the higher realms of self.

Item 32. Higher Levels of Self

Purpose: To find ways to access cosmic energies through the self.

In the following illustration, we see the four parts of the self and the deeper levels that can be obtained. As you delve into the higher levels of each one, they begin to point to the same end result (marked as the fourth level), which is unity. Different people are able to access higher levels in different ways. Some may be better at reaching unity through the mind, but wonder why they still do not feel connected. The reason may be that other parts of the self are still stuck on lower levels.

To reach a true state of unity, all parts of the self must transcend beyond their separate levels. When one can succeed in doing this, he or she will have a connection to a power beyond the self.

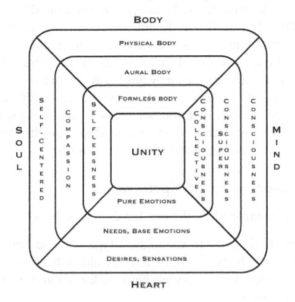

Higher Levels of Self

But how does one access this power? This is the purpose of ritual and meditation. The act of engaging in ritual is to separate one's self from the normal world and enter into one beyond. By concentrating on a magickal goal or even by just concentrating on your breath or a candle flame, you can experience that part of you that is beyond your single individuality. By meditating through dance, drumming, movement, singing, or just sitting, the attention is directed beyond the physical body. By forgiving those who have hurt you (meaning letting go of the hurt while still protecting yourself) and by seeking love without desiring anything in return, you elevate your heart to a higher level of openness and understanding, and by finding the inner self that is part of the universal self, a higher level of spiritual understanding is attained. If you can incorporate these things into your ritual practice, then you should be able to access deeper levels of understanding and power. But remember this: Magick is the act of willful transformation and the one entity that you can most influence through transformation is yourself. If you seek to do magick to influence another person, you are not acting to access higher levels of the self, you are seeking personal gratification. There is nothing wrong with wanting and needing things, but you must take time to understand why you desire such things. Magick, divination, and healing are never done BY you, they are done THROUGH you. If you do not succeed at your attempt to gain something, then it may be possible that it was not really meant for you to have. With each successful or unsuccessful act, there is a cosmic lesson to learn. Positive magick may not always seem to work, but it will always have a positive effect. Seek to gain what you truly need by first transforming yourself so that you become the type of person with the type of energy that will attract what you need to yourself. The following are some principles of spellcraft that I try to follow.

Item 33. Principles of Spellcraft

Purpose: An example of guidelines for doing spellwork.

- Try to limit spells to the highest types—those that aid or heal the highest self, or to offer aid or healing to others who choose to seek help, or for aid and healing for the earth.
- Cast spells only as the final effort to direct your will. First, do all that is within your physical, mental, and emotional ability to attain your goal before you begin magick.
- Spells for attainment of things not truly needed limit spiritual power and require karmic resolution.
- Spells that cause harm or pain to the self or others result in karmic resolution (see the Threefold Law, page 67).

The highest levels, or the types of spellcraft that are most likely to succeed, are those that involve aiding things beyond the self such as asking for healing for others. The lower forms of spellcraft, and the types that are least likely to succeed, are those involving personal desires—especially those desires that involve petty gain. If you can understand the concept that magick is done through you, then you can also understand the need to thank the gods if what you have done appears successful. If you receive, then give something in return.

For example, if you were to ask for money to help pay your bills and you received what you desired, use some of that money to help someone else. When you help others, you are making the world a slightly better place and you are returning your thanks to the cosmos. This will also help to ensure that your future work will be successful. The following chart lists some types of spells, whether or not something should be given back in return (karmic resolution), and the representative color associated with that type of work. This color can be used as the color for the working candle in the southern end of the altar, if you wish.

Item 34. Levels of Spells

Purpose: To determine particular types of spells and the need for karmic resolution, and for choosing a type of candle color for your altar (color used for working candle).

White

+ Used for ritualistic purposes.
+ Requires no resolution except a return of energies.

Purple

+ Used for rites of Initiation.
+ Used for spiritual contact.
+ Requires no karmic resolution.

Blue

+ Used for spiritual attainment for the self or others.
+ Used for the aid or healing for the self.
+ Used for aid or healing for others in need.
+ Used for aid or healing for other creatures in need.
+ Requires no karmic resolution.

Black

+ Used for absorption of negative energies.
+ Requires no karmic resolution.

Green

- Used for aid or healing for living plants and trees.
- Requires no karmic resolution.

Brown

- Used for aid or healing for the earth.
- Requires no karmic resolution.

Yellow

- Used for protection.
- Used for attainment of needs for self.
- Used for attainment of needs expressed by others.
- Requires an act of gratitude.

Red

- Used for protection.
- Used for attainment of desires for self or others.
- Requires karmic resolution.

The procedure in Item 35 can be used as a sample ritual for spellwork. The ritual work uses the four elements as points of focused thought and contemplation. Using this method helps to make you sure of your purpose and intent for the spellwork.

Item 35. Ritual for Spellwork

Purpose: An example of a procedure for spellwork.

1. Prepare your space and yourself.
2. State your intention and light a candle relating to the type of spell.
3. Banish and purify your space.
4. Cast the circle.
5. Set the four quadrants.
6. Invoke your deities.

7. Call the layers.
8. Begin the ritual.

   Face each quadrant separately and think about the implication of each on your goal:

   ♦ Face East (Air): Clearly visualize your goal.
     Be sure of your intent and reasons.

   ♦ Face South (Fire): Put your feelings into your goal.
     Be sure of feelings and the effects of this goal on others.

   ♦ Face West (Water): Invoke the aid of your deities.
     Be sure of the morality of the goal (remember the Rede).

   ♦ Face North (Earth): Do the physical work you have planned for your goal (candles, oils, etc.).
     Be sure of the effect of this goal on the earth and its creatures.

9. End the ritual and open your circle in reverse order.
10. Ground yourself.

For this ritual, use the standard ritual procedure you have developed so far. When you get to the main work, you will call upon each element to assist you. Face East and clearly visualize in your mind what you wish to happen. Say, for example, that you are doing a ritual to help you deliver an important speech. Clearly visualize in your mind an image of you speaking before the group with confidence and clarity. If you have trouble doing this, it may be because some fear or doubt exists within you. Ask for guidance to root out this mental block and continue your visualization. When you see the image clearly in your mind, then face South. Concentrate on your feelings and energies. Place these into the visualization of your goal. You should be able to not only see yourself accomplishing the goal, you should now also be able to feel it. Again, if you have trouble doing this, you may have an emotional block that you will need to clear. Ask for guidance and persist until a strong positive sense of action comes through. Next, face West and concentrate on the spirituality of your goal. Feel a connection with your deities or with the energy of the universe. Visualize how your goal will benefit the universe in some small but important way. All positive acts benefit the universe. Invoke the help of your deities to aid you in accomplishing your goal. Feel that energy fill you. Finally, face North and do the physical act of magick you wish to do to help you with your need. There are many methods of magick that you can use: crystal magick, cord magick, candle magick, etc. Remember, it is not the physical objects you are using that will do the work for you. They are only material objects that symbolize your own inner work. Use these tools to focus and direct these energies you have raised and to symbolize the visualizations you have enacted. Send your energy out into the universe so that it may be used by the cosmos to aid in your need or send the energies into a particular object. What you do physically depends on which method of magickal work you wish to do. Study several different methods until you find one with which you are most comfortable.

When you are through with your work, release the layers, deities, and the four elements in the reverse order in which you called upon them. Similarly, open your circle in the reverse direction and announce that your ritual is through. As before, be sure that you ground yourself by releasing the energy you have raised back into the earth.

The Basics of Meditation

An important part of ritual and magick work is meditation. Meditation is one of the easiest and most difficult spiritual practices. The basic goal of most meditative practices is to learn to just sit. This sounds easy enough. After all, who does not know how to sit? The difficulty is being able to just sit for a long period of time without letting the mind wander. It is like the practice of "breaking" a horse. A wild horse is not very keen on the idea of having another animal ride on its back. In order to turn a wild horse into a riding horse, it must be conditioned to allow a human to get on its back. In order to "break" the wild horse, someone has to get on it and just sit. But just sitting on a bucking bronco is no easy task. The mind is similar to a wild horse. It is always running off in different directions. It rides along the path of whatever thought that comes along. It likes to stay on the move and it certainly does not want to just sit still for a long period of time. The mind, too, has to be "broken" so that it can come under your control. It takes a great deal of practice and determination to have this sort of control over the mind. But it is that sort of control that is necessary for magickal work. The greatest tool of any

Wiccan is not any of those sitting on the altar, it is the mind. Access and control of the mind will yield more power than any oil or incense.

There are three elements to good meditative practice. Though there are many ways to practice meditation and many spiritual sources and traditions offer a variety of techniques, all the techniques have three common goals: relaxation, concentration, and absorption.

Relaxation

To begin any meditative practice, you must first be in a relaxed state of mind, body, heart, and soul. Let's begin with the body. Relaxing the body is best done through stretching and the release of tension. The physical practices of yoga and other body-stretching exercises are great ways to make your body flexible. Tension most often is stored in our muscles. By stretching these muscles, we can release this tension, increase flexibility, and strengthen our bodies. Before beginning any meditative practice, it is a good idea to stretch as much as possible. This also helps to alleviate the strain of sitting in one position for a long time. When you are ready to sit, concentrate on releasing tension throughout the body. One way to do this is to tense each muscle separately and tightly, and then quickly release that tension. After doing this, concentrate on sending warmth and relaxation throughout your body. Imagine if you could fill your body slowly from your feet upward with a warm and heavy liquid such as wax. Connect your breathing to your sitting. Imagine that each time you breathe in, you bring into your body warmth and relaxation, and every time you breathe out, you release tension from deep within your body. Next, encourage relaxation with the other parts of your self. Allow your mind to relax. Imagine that it feels as warm and relaxed as your body. Imagine that your mind is like an attic on a warm summer day. On each end of the attic are windows. Open those windows and allow the summer breeze to fill the room. Imagine that all your thoughts are like the breeze. Allow them simply to come into the room in one window and drift out the other window. Do not think about each thought. Let each drift silently by. Encourage emotional relaxation by allowing this special meditation time to be a gift to yourself. Accept yourself for who you are. You are a developing and progressing being, and at this moment in time, allow yourself to be exactly who you are. During this time, remember that you do not have to be anything special to anyone else. You can be completely and fully yourself. Finally, allow the gods to enter into your soul and fill you with happiness, wisdom, and guidance.

Concentration

The next element of meditation is concentration. Each spiritual tradition that uses meditation has different objects of concentration, but the principle is the same. Focus your mind on an object or idea for a long period of time. Do not allow your mind to wander. If it does, relax again and gently start over. Your mind will be like the wild horse that will want to run off. Grab the wild beast by the reins and pull it back into the ring. Do not be harsh with yourself. Making judgments about your abilities is not helpful and further impedes your concentration. Simply begin again without comment.

The object of concentration can be any number of things. It can be visual such as the flame of a candle, a crystal, a special symbol, or a drawing or artwork. You can concentrate on repeating a word or phrase in your mind. If you are working with a chant or power word, you might repeat that. You can concentrate on a sound or some piece of music. Some people concentrate on their breathing or just on silence itself. Whatever you choose, focus on it for a period of time. Try five minutes at first, and then work up to at least 20 minutes. In magickal practice, it is often important to learn how to visualize. You can practice meditation by concentrating on visualizing something in your mind. Try to maintain your vision of the object just as if your eyes were open and you were staring at it.

Absorption

The final stage of meditation is the most difficult. If you can maintain concentration for at least 20 minutes or more, you may be able to reach a state of mind where you become absorbed and merge with your object of concentration. You completely lose the sense of self and enter into a state of being in which the object and the viewer are part of the same eternal reality. It is here that the wild horse is finally tamed. But, more than that, there is no longer a rider and a horse, there is only that which is both rider and horse. One who has learned to reach this stage of meditation learns to peer into the minds of the gods.

These are the basics of most passive meditative practices. You should begin to develop a regular meditation routine to develop your powers of concentration and visualization. Later degrees of this system involve a great deal of meditation on different objects and ideas. By developing a consistent and regular practice, you will be able to practice future meditations with little difficulty. Start to set aside a special time every day in which you can regularly meditate. If you cannot do it every day, try to set aside at least one day a week.

Basic Meditation

Let's take a look at a very basic meditation that can be used for Wiccan practice. First, make your meditation space sacred by drawing a circle around yourself. I often begin by facing each direction and saying a small invocation. Next, do some stretches. Try to cover most, if not all, of the major muscle groups. Then, sit. I often place a stone in each of the four directions of my circle to mark my sacred space. Begin to relax your mind and body. Find something to concentrate your thoughts on, such as a candle or an image of your deity. You can use an actual object or symbol, or you can visualize something in your mind. Focus your thoughts on this object for a few moments. Enjoy the peacefulness and silence. Enjoy the chance to do something good for yourself. Be thankful for being alive and well, and feel the love and power of the God and Goddess within you. When you are through, be sure to ground yourself by hugging the earth (or something connected to the earth). Rise up and thank the gods and the four elements and directions.

The Basics of Healing

Healing and divination are also important aspects of the Craft. This is where the practitioner allows the forces of the Cosmos, or the gods, to work through him or her in order to help others. Just as in spellcasting, the principles of learning to do these acts requires years of study and practice.

Before you begin to study healing, however, a common misconception must be rectified. Though our society likes to stress that only experts can do certain things such as healing and counseling, this is not entirely true. We are all capable, to some degree, of healing ourselves and others. I am not advocating that you never see your doctor. Western medicine has advanced greatly in the understanding and treatment of the human body, but it has not explored very well the connection between mind and body. If you or others are in need of medical attention, by all means, get that attention as soon as possible. But do not accept that only professionals can affect changes in your body. You have the ability to control and alter many things within yourself through the power of your mind and through magick. That is what magick is all about—willful transformation. Healing can occur with yourself through the use of physical objects and through concentration of the mind.

Methods of Healing

There are many methods of healing. Item 36 provides a list of some of them. As a practicing Wiccan, you should choose at least one of the methods and begin to *study* it. This does not necessarily mean that you should begin practicing such a method. Many of these methods require years of study with a professional tutor.

Item 36. Methods of Healing

Purpose: Identify different methods in order to choose at least one to study.

acupressure:	Pressure applied to body pressure points.
acupuncture:	Needles inserted in body meridians.
aromatherapy:	Therapy through specific smells.
aura visioning:	Seeing the shape and condition of auras.
Bach flowers:	Specific flower treatments.
color healing:	Healing through the use of specific colors.
energy healing:	Healing through manipulating energies.
homeopathy:	Healing hrough the application of very minute amounts of material similar in substance to the original cause of the infliction.
herbology:	Healing through the use of herbs.
reflexology:	Massage of specific areas of the feet.
radiesthesia:	Healing through pendulums.

Healers take many, many years of guided study and practice before they become skilled at working with others. If your goal is to become a healer, then you should consider the same amount of effort taken in conjunction with a skilled teacher. As a developing first degree Wiccan, it is not our purpose to become healers—that is a separate practice—but we can come to understand the process of healing and let that understanding become part of our spiritual training. Choose one of the methods as a means of understanding alternative forms of healing. Through the study of healing principles, you may come to understand the connections of mind, body, spirit, and emotions in the regulation of a healthy self.

The Chakras

Central to almost all methods of spiritual healing is an understanding of the main energy points in the body known as the chakras. Chakra literally means "wheel," and it is believed that these seven places in the body are power centers that spin with vital energy. These centers connect the physical body to other, less dense bodies. This constant free-flow is an important part of maintaining health in our bodies. Many conditions of ill health can be created by imbalances in the energies flowing through us. Each of the seven main chakras (there are many other chakras, such as those in the palms of the hands) has an expression in the body, a color, and a sound through which it can be accessed or focused on.

Item 37. The Chakras

Purpose: Learn places of energy for healing.

Root Center

Number:	1
Expression:	basic survival
Color:	red
Sound:	hmm
Location:	base of spine
Keywords:	feeling connected to the earth, grounding, material conditions

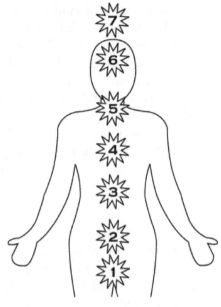

The Chakras

Sexual Center

Number:	2
Expression:	propagation
Color:	orange
Sound:	hee
Location:	just below navel
Keywords:	sexual blocks or dysfunctions, life force, creativity

Navel Center

Number:	3
Expression:	the will
Color:	yellow
Sound:	heh
Location:	solar plexus
Keywords:	vitalizes physical and etheric bodies, issues of power and control, energy, willpower

Heart Center

Number:	4
Expression:	the emotions
Color:	green/pink
Sound:	huh
Location:	center of chest
Keywords:	love and compassion, centeredness and balance, harmony, synthesis

Throat Center

Number:	5
Expression:	communication
Color:	light blue
Sound:	hoh
Location:	throat
Keywords:	develops clairaudience, proper speech, center of headaches, tension

Third Eye

Number:	6
Expression:	thoughts, psychic
Color:	purple
Sound:	hah
Location:	middle of forehead
Keywords:	develops clairvoyance, clear thinking

Crown

Number:	7
Expression:	spiritual
Color:	white
Sound:	aum
Location:	top of head
Keywords:	develops sense of connection to spiritual oneness

The Aura

Another common concept discussed in most methods of spiritual healing is the energy field known as the aura. This is a band (or several combined bands) of energy that surrounds the human body. Some have the ability to actually see this band of energy. The aura may be reflected in bands of various colors. Each of these colors describes conditions of the aura. This, in turn, helps to describe the state of health of the person to whom the aura is connected. Being able to see or sense this aura on living beings can help the healer to determine the condition and cause of a person's illness.

Item 38. The Aura

Purpose: Learn about this field of energy for healing.

The Basics of Divination

Divination is the ability to assess a person's state of being and the state of energies that are involved in a person's life in order to determine a likely turn of events. Divination is not fortune telling. No one is capable of seeing the future for certain because there is no certain singular future. There exists only a range of possibilities—some of which are more likely to occur than others. By understanding a current condition of energies and influences, one can assess the most likely possibilities that exist. If, for example, I was to stand on the edge of a busy street corner, close my eyes, and proceed to walk across the street amidst the traffic, you might be able to accurately predict that I may get hit by a car. You know from past experience that such things are possible and likely on a busy street. Conditions could change, of course. I might realize my foolish mistake and open my eyes in time to escape being hit, or the traffic may suddenly stop. It is more likely, however, that I will be hit by a car. This process of determining the most likely outcomes for any situation is the same for divination because you are able to look at a range of possibilities and can get an idea of a possible outcome. Knowing these possible outcomes can help you or others make decisions about the future.

Methods of Divination

Divination can be done instantly by those who have special abilities such as clairvoyance or other supramental powers. For others, tools are needed to create symbols and patterns from which a reader can determine conditions. This is often done through methods of chance. This may, at first, seem odd. How can pure random events create significant meanings? Chance may not be as purely random as we may believe. Chaos theory and the understanding of subatomic physics has revised our notion of pure randomness. Chance events are influenced by those who partake in chance selections. In other words, every time we engage in a chance activity (such as rolling dice), we influence the outcomes in some small manner. It is also believed that the gods can reveal information through chance events. Even if you found it impossible to believe in any of these ideas about chance, you can still believe in its power when you consider that a chance event can help the reader to find a deeper understanding of a situation by finding connections between seemingly unrelated symbols and information that is only possible through chance.

There are many tools that can help to create these chance events. Some of these are listed in Item 39. Some of them are common methods, while some are quite obscure yet interesting to note. All involve some sort of prediction through a method of choosing an interpretation from a range of possibilities—mostly through chance. Many of the methods of predictions use the creation and relationship of preformed or formed symbols. Understanding the significance of the symbols is the key to determining possible answers.

Below is listed several common and some not-so-common techniques for practicing divination.

Item 39. Methods of Divination

Purpose: Choose a method of divination to study.

aeromancy:
: A method of determining the future by observing various atmospheric conditions.

alectryomancy:
: A bird is encouraged to pick grain from a circle of letters. The letters chosen then determine words or phrases for predictions.

aleuromancy:
: Balls of dough are baked. Common answers to questions such as yes or no are placed in each one. A question is asked and then a ball is chosen for the answer.

astrology:
: Predictions of current and future conditions are made based on the alignments of planets within the solar system and within zodiac star patterns.

belomancy:
: A method of prediction done through the tossing of arrows. The direction and placement of the fallen arrows creates patterns and indicative directions.

capnomancy:
: Smoke rising from fires is observed for possible patterns.

cartomancy:
: A very popular method of observing patterns made by combinations of playing or special cards. The use of a tarot deck is a method of cartomancy.

ceroscopy:
: Hot wax poured into cold water can create special shapes and images.

crystallomancy:
: A method of prediction done through reading crystals and the shapes and images that appear within.

dice reading:
: Conditions are read by the numbers that are rolled with dice.

geomancy:	Predictions are made by reading sand markings or images in natural objects.
gyromancy:	People form a circle over a circle of letters marked on the ground, and the people swirl until they fall down.
graphology:	The shapes and lines of handwriting are observed.
I Ching:	An ancient Chinese method of observing patterns of yin and yang through the tossing of sticks or coins.
numerology:	Conditions are read according to numbers. Personal information such as names, birthdays, dates, etc., are converted into numbers that can then be interpreted.
oneiromancy:	Dreams and their interpretations are the basis of this method of divination.
palmistry:	A very old method of reading lines and patterns in the palm of a hand.
pyromancy:	Through the actions of a burning candle, patterns of prediction can be made.
radiesthesia:	The most popular method of this type of divination is to hold a pendulum between the fingers. The direction of the pendulum's swing provides answers to questions.
runes:	Answers are sought through ancient alphabetical systems.
scrying:	Gazing into a reflective surface such as a special mirror or crystal ball encourages patterns to be seen.
tasseography:	This is another ancient method that creates meaningful symbols with patterns of tea leaves used when drinking tea.

Basic Tarot Cards

One of the most popular forms of divination is done through the use of tarot cards. No one is really certain as to when tarot cards first appeared, but they do seem to have a connection to ancient wisdom.

The cards are popular because they are rich in beautiful images and symbolism, which can lead to variety of possible readings and understandings. However, this richness can make the cards seem a bit daunting to learn at first. Because the tarot is so popular, I will offer a bit of introduction to them. Like any method of healing or divination, the tarot requires continuous study.

To begin the study of the tarot, notice that there are three major divisions of the deck: the minor arcana (usually has an Arabic numeral and a suit, such as the 3 of Wands), the court cards (usually has a royal title and a suit, such as the Queen of Swords), and major arcana cards (usually has a Roman numeral and a title with no suit, such as XXI The Fool). The minor arcana cards deal with everyday common energies, the court cards usually deal with people in our lives or they can deal with mixed energies, and the major arcana cards deal with strong forces acting in a person's life.

When reading tarot cards, they are usually placed in a formation called a *spread*. Each position in the spread is concerned with different aspects or conditions of a reading. To determine a complete reading, you must understand what each card means in relation to its position and to its relationship with the other cards in the spread. First, begin by understanding the possibilities available in each card. It must be remembered that each card has several possible meanings or interpretations. Most tarot decks come with a book explaining the meanings of each card, but I suggest that you do not limit yourself to only the meanings provided in the book. Learn to interpret all the symbols available on each card. For example, with the minor arcana cards, I often use the meanings of the numbers and the suits along with any symbols and words revealed on the card. All of these things combined will give the reader a variety of reading possibilities. The correct choice in the possibilities will be revealed by comparing that card to the others in the spread, and will also depend on the question or purpose of the reading.

Begin with an understanding of the numbers. Each number from 1 to 10 has a special meaning. If you study the Qaballah, a mystical study developed from the practices of Judaism, you will learn that the numbers from 1 to 10 actually reveal a story of the creation of the universe from the one source to the creation of humankind and their lessons. Here is a simplified version of my understanding of the numbers and their meanings.

Item 40. The Meanings of Numbers

Purpose: Can be used to interpret meanings in the tarot and numerology.

Number	Story of Creation	Meaning
Ace	The one true essence comes into existence.	beginning, purity
2	The one looks for itself and divides into two opposites.	change, division, separation
3	The two create life.	reunion, balance, birth, creation, short travel
4	A home is created for life to inhabit.	foundations, home, meetings, long travel
5	Humankind is created but greed creates sadness and loss.	cycles, loss, humanity
6	Humankind learns the lesson of loss and regain.	learning, insight, gain, expansion
7	Humankind learns about personal and spiritual love.	spirituality, mystery, luck, love, spirit, philosophy
8	Death and rebirth is created to ensure change and renewal.	achievements, infinity, cycle of birth/death, health
9	Creation and learning is accomplished.	completion, ending, resolution
10	A new direction in creation and learning begins.	commitment, a new start

In the reading of a minor arcana card, the meaning of the number is then combined with the meaning of the suit. There are four suits in the standard tarot deck, each of which is related to one of the four elements previously studied. The standard four suits and their possible relationships are shown in Item 41.

Item 41. The Four Suits

Purpose: Understand the meanings of the elements in tarot cards.

Swords (Air):   thinking, communication, mental health, visualization, travel

Wands (Fire):   outer emotions, relationships, life energy, emotional health

Cups (Water):   inner emotions, spirituality, alternative healing

Disks (Earth):   physical, financial, business, physical health

These, of course, are my interpretations of the four suits and are related to my own understanding of the four elements and their relationship to the human personality. Swords (such as the athame) cut through the air, so this suit relates to the element of Air. It is the realm of thoughts and visualizations. Thoughts conveyed to another become communication, and because communication involves the movement of one idea from one place to another, air also deals with travel and movement. Wands are the pieces of wood that hold the flame of a torch. Thus, wands are related to the element of Fire. Fire, to me, represents the life energy we all possess, and that energy is manifested through our actions expressed from within outwardly to others. We often feel one way inside, but express ourselves differently on the outside. Outwardly, we are concerned with how our actions will be interpreted by others in our many relationships. Our true inner emotions come under the realm of the element of Water. (Still waters run deep!) Cups are used to symbolize Water because they are meant to hold liquids. Liquid and fluid are also great descriptions of our true secret inner emotions. Sometimes, at the expense of our own health, we do not express our true emotions, but they are nonetheless there and influence our actions from deep within. The fourth suit, Disks, relates to the coins we call change or money. They represent the earthly physical existence we experience every day. As physical beings we must eat, sleep, and have shelter in order to survive, and all those things take money and physical effort.

To further your understanding of the meanings of tarot cards, combine the meanings of the numbers with the suits and any other information available on the card. For example, the 3 of Swords may be interpreted as meaning the creation (3) of a new idea (Swords).

The art on the card may help to reinforce that idea or it may give further meaning to the possibility. It would then be necessary to compare this possible reading to the possible readings of the other cards seen in the spread.

Another type of card in the tarot deck, the court card, often describes the influences or actions of other people in our lives.

Item 42. Meanings of the Court Cards

Purpose: Understanding these cards in tarot readings.

Princess (Earth):   young female or earth influence
Prince (Air):   young male or air influence
Knight (Fire):   older male or fire influence
Queen (Water):   older female or water influence

Relate the court card to the suit with which it appears. For example, the Prince of Wands may be interpreted as representing a young man (Prince) who is very emotional or who has a lot of energy (Wands). The representation of a person may be more symbolic than real. Consider the energies of male versus female in humans, and then consider what they might represent. For example, in the Prince of Wands, the Prince might represent a young, aggressive energy rather than an actual person. Looking at the spread and comparing the card to the other cards around it will help determine the correct interpretation. Also, don't be afraid to ask if the card could represent a real person or something more symbolic. Notice that each court card is also related to one of the four elements. If the presence of a person does not make sense in a reading, then the court card may be related to mixed energies. For example, the Prince of Wands may be interpreted as Earth (Prince) in Fire (Wands). Earth in Fire could mean a physical act (Earth) that is full of energy or aggression (Fire).

Finally, the major arcana cards often relate to major forces at play in a person's life. Each major arcana can also have a variety of meanings, but they often are related to the qualities developed in a person who is on a spiritual journey. All the minor arcana and the court cards are related to one of the four suits—the four elements. The major arcana is related to the fifth element—Spirit. The following list gives a simplified version of some possible meanings, but explore to find further meanings as well.

Item 43. The Major Arcana

Purpose: Understand meanings of the major arcana cards in a tarot reading.

Fool:	beginning the journey
Magus:	seeking the spiritual male (God)
Priestess:	seeking the spiritual female (Goddess)
Empress:	seeking the earthly female (mother)
Emperor:	seeking the earthly male (father)
Hierophant:	becoming the teacher, alchemist
Lovers:	learning unselfishness, balance, love
Chariot:	learning perseverance, direction, take control
Adjustment:	learning understanding, fairness, decision, justice
Hermit:	learning introspection, silence, meditation
Fortune:	learning about flexibility, luck, the wheel of cycles
Lust:	learning to overcome overt desire
Hanged Man:	learning modesty, sacrifice, how to see a different view
Death:	learning about ending, renewal
Art:	learning about creativity, reworking, combining
Devil:	becoming the trickster, joker
Tower:	overcoming old ways, old obstacle
Star:	developing sincerity, hope, discovering hidden wisdom
Moon:	developing gentleness, intuition, feminine qualities
Sun:	developing strength, growth, male qualities
Aeon:	developing patience, making wise decisions, seeking a new era
Universe:	incorporating wholeness, union

To begin the practice of reading tarot cards, start by separating your deck into the three divisions: minor arcana cards, major arcana cards, and court cards. Shuffle each of the three piles. Begin with the minor arcana cards. Turn over one card and practice interpreting at least three possible meanings for that card. Remember to use all the information available to you on the card. After learning the minor arcana, do the same with the court cards, and then the major arcana cards as well. Then, start practicing with multiple cards by doing a three card spread. Shuffle the entire deck together, and then choose three cards. Place them in a line.

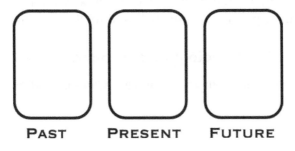

PAST   **PRESENT**   **FUTURE**

Three Card Spread

The center card describes the present situation. The card on the left describes how that situation came to be (the past), while the card on the right describes where the situation might lead (the future). Practice interpreting these cards separately and then together. Read the three cards together as if they were presenting a story line.

After learning to do this, learn other possible spreads and practice using them until you find one that works well for you. You can even make up your own spreads to suit your own purposes.

Basic Astrology

Astrology is the art of observing energies represented by the 10 planets (the sun and moon used to be considered planets rather than a star and a satellite, so the eight planets of the solar system along with the sun and moon are called the 10 planets) combined with the 12 constellations that fall along a particular line known as the line of the zodiac. A person's astrological chart illustrates where the 10 planets were located in relation to the zodiac on the day and time of that person's birth. By observing the location of these planets, one can determine particular forces of energy that were at work during the time of birth that are believed to be of significant influence throughout a person's life. Most people are familiar with their sun sign—that is, the astrological sign in which the sun would have appeared (to us on earth) on the day of a person's birth. The sun is only one of the 10 planets, however, and additional information can be obtained by observing the location of the other planets as well. Item 44 shows the 12 sun signs and some associations. Again, these are the associations that I have developed and which work for me. Not all of them are considered the standard associations. For example, Gemini is usually considered related to the color of blue or yellow, Virgo to grey or green, and the zodiac sign Libra is usually linked to blue or pink.

Item 44. The Astrological Sun Signs

Purpose: Determine your own sun sign. Can be used as representations of others.

Aries

Number:	1
Date:	March 21–April 20
Ruling Planet:	Mars
Color:	red
Element:	Fire
Energy:	cardinal
Keywords:	straightforward, self-centered, passionate, active, leader, bold, resourceful

Taurus

Number:	2
Date:	April 21–May 20
Ruling Planet:	Venus
Color:	pink
Element:	Earth
Energy:	fixed
Keywords:	perseverent, stubborn, patient, sensual, artistic, persistent, strong presence

Gemini

Number:	3
Date:	May 21–June 21
Ruling Planet:	Mercury
Color:	green
Element:	Air
Energy:	mutable
Keywords:	versatile, intellectual, moody, malleable, childlike

Cancer

Number:	4
Date:	June 22–July 22
Ruling Planet:	moon
Color:	white
Element:	Water
Energy:	cardinal
Keywords:	nurturing, emotional, imaginative, sensitive, kind, possessive, home-centered

Leo

Number:	5
Date:	July 23–August 23
Ruling Planet:	sun
Color:	yellow
Element:	Fire
Energy:	fixed
Keywords:	active, powerful, loyal, flamboyant, firm, optimistic, ambitious

Virgo

Number:	6
Date:	August 24–September 22

Ruling Planet: Mercury
Color: blue
Element: Earth
Energy: mutable
Keywords: detailed, dedicated, critical, dutiful, energetic

Libra

Number: 7
Date: September 23–October 22
Ruling Planet: Venus
Color: light brown
Element: Air
Energy: cardinal
Keywords: balanced, loves beauty, artistic, amiable, indecisive, fair, seeks justice

Scorpio

Number: 8
Date: October 23–November 22
Ruling Planet: Pluto
Color: dark red
Element: Water
Energy: fixed
Keywords: sarcastic, passionate, intense, curious, intuitive, industrious, pessimistic

Sagittarius

Number: 9
Date: November 23–December 21
Ruling Planet: Jupiter
Color: purple
Element: Fire

Energy: mutable
Keywords: loves freedom, seeks truth, outspoken, logical, intelligent, idealistic

Capricorn

Number: 10
Date: December 22–January 20
Ruling Planet: Saturn
Color: black
Element: Earth
Energy: cardinal
Keywords: materialistic, disciplined, controlling, worrier, persistent, challenging

Aquarius

Number: 11
Date: January 21–Febbruary 18
Ruling Planet: Uranus
Color: dark blue
Element: Air
Energy: fixed
Keywords: altruistic, original, unique, stubborn, compassionate, idealistic

Pisces

Number: 12
Date: February 19–March 20
Ruling Planet: Neptune
Color: green
Element: Water
Energy: mutable
Keywords: mystical, emotional, imaginative, artistic, withdrawn, moody, ambivalent

If you wish to determine the forces that were at work during your birth, you will need to obtain a natal chart that shows the location of all the planets during the exact date and time of your birth. Next, you will need to know what each of the 10 planets represents.

Item 45. The 10 Planets

Purpose: Observe energies represented by the planets as used in astrological charts.

Sun

Number:	1
Day:	Sunday
Color:	yellow
Sign:	Leo
Metal:	gold
Keywords:	the self, ego, fatherhood, outward appearance, strength, success

Moon

Number:	2
Day:	Monday
Color:	white
Sign:	Cancer
Metal:	silver
Keywords:	the emotions, instinct, nurturance, childbirth, motherhood

Mercury

Number:	3
Day:	Thursday
Color:	green
Sign:	Gemini
Metal:	mercury

Keywords: communication, the intellect, children, aware-
              ness, reasoning, short trips

Saturn

Number: 4
Day: Saturday
Color: black
Sign: Capricorn
Metal: lead
Keywords: discipline, responsibility, time, restrictions,
              perseverance, order, grandparents

Mars

Number: 5
Day: Tuesday
Color: red
Sign: Aries
Metal: steel
Keywords: energy, passion, aggression, assertion, sexuality,
              grandchildren

Jupiter

Number: 6
Day: Wednesday
Color: purple
Sign: Sagittarius
Metal: tin
Keywords: learning, spirituality, values, fortune, expansion,
              friends

Venus

Number: 7
Day: Friday

Color:	pink
Sign:	Libra
Metal:	copper
Keywords:	pleasure, love, money, partnerships, socializing, beauty, possessions, romantic relationship

Pluto

Number:	8
Day:	—
Color:	grey
Sign:	Scorpio
Metal:	alloys
Keywords:	transformation, regeneration, rebirth, death, obsession, the subconscious, those who have died

Neptune

Number:	9
Day:	—
Color:	blue
Sign:	Aquarius
Metal:	aluminum
Keywords:	illusion, mystery, mysticism, delusion, unknown people, long trips

Uranus

Number:	10
Day:	—
Color:	orange
Sign:	Taurus
Metal:	iron
Keywords:	expanded consciousness, rebellion, nonconformity, idealism, freedom, creativity, enemies

You will also need to learn about the 12 houses that are used in an astrological chart. The houses are the 12 locations of the zodiac in which the planets appear when we view them from the earth. Each house is related to an influence in our lives, such as money or relationships. The chart in Item 46 gives a basic keyword for each house.

Item 46. The 12 Astrological Houses

Purpose: Reading a natal chart.

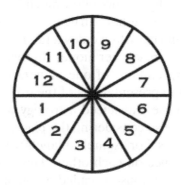

Astrological Houses

First House:	the self, personality
Second House:	possessions, values, money
Third House:	communication, intelligence, education
Fourth House:	home, roots, grounding, ancestry
Fifth House:	pleasure, creativity, romance, children
Sixth House:	health, work, service, daily concerns
Seventh House:	partnerships, emotional relationships
Eighth House:	sex, inheritance, death, rebirth
Ninth House:	philosophy, higher education, laws, travel
10th House:	social status, vacations, hobbies, social change
11th House:	friendships, desires, philanthropy
12th House:	subconscious, setbacks, hidden forces

To read a natal chart, observe the location of each planet in relation to the sign and house in which it resides. For example, a chart may contain the sun in Libra in the second house. By comparing the energies of the sun (self, personality, ego) with the sign of Libra (balanced, curious, artistic), you might determine that the person represented by the chart appears to be a very balanced person or you might determine that this person finds her sense of self through her artwork. Applying this information to the characteristics represented by the second house (possessions, values, money), you might determine that this person tends to be balanced in her financial affairs—she might be one that carefully balances how much is spent with an equal amount that is saved, making her a frugal person but one who does not hoard her money and can often enjoy a fun night out, or she might be an artist who actually makes her money through her art. These are just two possible interpretations of one planetary setting. The chart would also contain the representations of the other nine planets each within a sign and a house. Advanced astrology would include all of this information, while also considering the placements of the planets within the circle of houses. For example, planets within the same house have a particular influence on each other. This placement of two or more planets in the same house is called a conjunction. Other relationships are also observed based on how far other planets are from each other in the chart. For the beginning astrologer, however, plenty of information can be gained by just observing the planets in their positions.

The Runes

Another popular method of divination is the use of the runes, which were discussed on pages 64–65. Not only is each rune a letter that can be used as a script for writing, each also has a special significance. Like the tarot, readings can be made by drawing runes (through stones or cards) and determining the meaning of that rune in relation to the question asked and whether or not additional runes are drawn (as in a tarot spread). Item 47 shows the meanings most commonly given to the runes.

Item 47. The Runes and Their Meanings

Purpose: For divination and making sigils.

Rune	Name	Letter	Meaning
ᚠ	Fehu	f	fire, wealth, material needs, goals, promotion
ᚢ	Uruz	u	house, desire, inner feelings, unconscious
ᚦ	Thurisaz	th	thorn, hardship, pain, introspection, focus
ᚨ	Ansuz	a	air, leader, justice, teacher, intelligence, communication
ᚲ	Kenaz	k	knowledge, wisdom, insight, creativity, inspiration
ᚷ	Gebo	g	gift, love, marriage, partnership
ᚹ	Wunjo	w,v	joy, success, recognition, contentment
ᚱ	Raido	r	ride, journey, change, destiny, travel
ᚺ	Hagalaz	h	hailstorm, loss, destruction, change
ᚾ	Nauthiz	n	need, poverty, hardship, responsibility, frustration
ᛁ	Isa	i	ice, block, stagnant, patience, rest
ᛃ	Yera	y	year, change, cycle, rewards, motion
ᛇ	Eihwaz	j	junction, endings, transformation, death, rebirth
ᛈ	Pertho	p	pawn, magic, mystery, prophecy, chance, work
ᛉ	Algiz	x,z	protection, assistance
ᛊ	Sowulo	s	sun, strength, positive energy, activity, conscious, male
ᛏ	Tiwaz	t	truth, struggle, duty, discipline, warrior, justice, god
ᛒ	Berkana	b	birth, growth, health, earth
ᛖ	Ehwaz	e	equality, duality, change, love, partnerships
ᛗ	Mannaz	m	mankind, human, self, family, humanity
ᛚ	Laguz	l	lake, water, emotion, fears, female
ᛜ	Inguz	ng	energy, sex, work, grounding, balance, land
ᛞ	Dagaz	d	day, happiness, success, time
ᛟ	Othila	o	goddess, property, home, permanance, legacy, moon

In the same manner as the tarot cards, pieces of stone or wood with rune signs added can be pulled from a bag or other container at random (whether there is true randomness is another matter). A spread of one or more runes can be created. Just as you may have done with the tarot cards, try a spread of three runes in a straight line and use them to represent past, present, and future. As before, interpret a story line as created by the three runes. Another method is to select nine runes from the bag (nine is a very significant number in Norse mythology). Throw those nine runes onto a table. Observe which ones are face up, remove any that are face down, and also observe where the runes have landed in relation to each other. Make a reading based on these patterns.

Additional Practices

The following are some suggested additional things you might do in relation to the completion of the first degree. These activities include finding yourself a magickal name, reading additional books related to the topics discussed in this section, beginning some study in the arts to further personal expression, and looking into the martial arts as a means to study body-mind connections.

Many Pagans create and use a magickal name for themselves. In fact, some have many names. One can be used as a pen name or a name that is shared within a Pagan group, while another can be a private name that is used only in ritual work. There are a variety of ways these names can be discovered, but it's important that you feel they represent you and your beliefs. Find a name or set of names and a sigil that feels right to you. Then, consecrate them with a ritual.

All the subjects presented in this chapter are merely introductions to many branches of magickal study. You should consider reading and studying books related to these subjects, as well as any other books about the Craft, mysticism, spellcasting, ritual, divination, healing, or any other similar subjects. Enter each book you read into your listing in your BoW.

Exploring an art or craft is an excellent way to learn to play and be expressive. Learning the ways of Wicca involves a great deal of right-brain thinking activities, such as the use of intuition and creativity. Learning and practicing an art is a great way to help develop these faculties.

Forget about the result of your work; that does not matter. It is not about doing it right! It is the practice of doing the art that develops your abilities. If you are not having fun creating, then you cannot truly be expressive. We are taught to believe that the product is more important than the process. With your own creativity, this is not the case.

Many martial arts are actually mystical practices in motion. Especially interesting practices include t'ai chi and aikido. These and other forms discuss ways in which energies can be moved and manipulated and are very worthwhile physical and mental exercises for the developing Wiccan. Consider looking into one of these mystical arts.

Initiation to First Degree

You have learned a great deal and now it is time to recognize your achievements. First, review your progress of what you have accomplished so far. Review all your notes in your journal and write a final note to close it out.

Once you have completed your review and believe that you are ready to accept the level of first degree, write a first degree Initiation ceremony that is meaningful to you. Be sure to cast a circle and implement the things you have learned about ritual and ceremony. Mark the date of your Initiation because further study requires a year and a day of work beyond that date.

Congratulations, Maid or Squire! You are now a Wiccan Practitioner! Attach a yellow cord to your pendant and celebrate! You are now ready to begin work on the second degree.

Chapter 3

The Second Degree: Path of the Heart

- ⚘ Number: 2
- ⚘ Title: Wiccan Priest or Priestess
- ⚘ Prefix: Mistress or Master
- ⚘ Color: red
- ⚘ Gift: lighter, candle, candleholder
- ⚘ Goals:
    1. Profess a desire to continue study of the Craft of Wicca. Explain to yourself in writing why you wish to commit to a year and a day of study for this degree.
    2. Pursue the first Great Mystery.
    3. Create second degree magick books.
    4. Create an inner temple.
    5. Enact meditations to open the seven main chakras.
    6. Enact the four elemental meditations.
    7. Enact meditations on the three deities.
    8. Enact symbolic meditations.
    9. Enact a ritual for the purpose of raising and directing energy.

10. Develop methods for aura sensing, cleansing, and protection.
11. Begin psychic work.
12. Teach others.
13. Write and enact an Initiation to second degree.

The second degree is about putting your knowledge into practice and exploring the mystical roots and mysteries upon which Wicca is based. Each practitioner, of course, will experience these mysteries differently, but with conviction and belief, something will be experienced. Most of all, allow the thinking part of you to step aside so that you may learn to feel. Intuition, feeling, and mystical experience are what are needed at this point in your progress. Trust your feelings, let the strange be normal, and be open to new awareness. The goal of this level is to seek universal love and learn to share and express it to others.

The First Great Mystery

Now that you have obtained the first degree, you have learned the basics of the Craft and are ready to delve into understanding the first Great Mystery. All the activities for the second degree are designed to take you beyond knowledge and into experience. Through all these activities, you should begin to feel a connection to something beyond and greater than yourself. The first Great Mystery to discover is determining what this power is. Your answer will be unique, for you are a unique being. You might experience a presence or a power that is not your own. You might encounter a being, an animal, a dream image, or an image of the Lord or Lady. You might simply hear other sounds or feel an unusual sensation. There are hundreds of ways of encountering the Divine. Let us, for now, call it the presence of the mysterious—the essence of the powers we have come to call God and Goddess. Allow yourself to experience this presence in the work that you do. It is not necessary that you completely understand it. It is more important to have the experience without explaining it and without denying its validity because it cannot be understood. That is why it is one of the Great Mysteries.

Celebrating the Cycles

As you work on this degree, remember also to continue to participate in the Wheel of the Year either through personal rituals or through participation in public rituals. For each sabbat, esbat, and astor, develop a ritual that relates to that particular celebration and which has meaning to you. There are many sources for finding rituals that others have written, and sometimes it helps to get ideas from other people, but the strongest rituals are those that are written by the practitioner. Let's take a look at an example of a ritual for each of these three types of celebrations to get an idea of how you might create your own rituals for each.

As you may recall from the first degree, the sabbat is a celebration of the cycles of the sun (actually, the cycles of the earth's revolution around the sun) and the qualities of the God. To create a sabbat ritual, refer to the characteristics of the God (page 45) and to the section about the cycles of the sun and the solar festivals (pages 62–63). You could also refer to the Call of the God (pages 42–43). Item 48 gives a sample of a ritual for Mabon (the start of fall) that incorporates these elements. After you are done with your sabbat, you might want to change the colors on your altar to reflect the new season.

Item 48. Sample Mabon Sabbat

Purpose: An example for designing a Mabon ritual.

1. Prepare your materials and altar.
2. State intention (light working candle).

   It is I, [state common or magickal name], who comes before thee to initiate this circle of power for the purpose I state: Tonight I celebrate the sabbat festival of Mabon— the Fall Equinox. On this day light and dark are balanced as the Wheel turns toward the dark part of the year. As the leaves of the trees fall in splendid color, as the air begins to chill, and as the light of the day begins to fade, it appears as if the great Sun God is fading. This is also the time of the final harvest—a time to look back upon works done and to be thankful for what I have. I come to celebrate Mabon. That is my intention.

3. Banish and purify.
4. Cast the circle.
5. Ritual.
   a. Read the Call of the God aloud.
   b. Enter your inner temple and begin a meditation (see page 137 for how to create your inner temple). Take some time to think about the blessings you have and be thankful.
   c. When you are through, read aloud the following honor to the God, then light a gold candle.

   O great sun, God entity

   the source of masculinity

   hear my words addressed to thee.

   I come before thee most reverently.

   In you I celebrate the selfless giving;

   to offer what I can to all those living.

   In you I celebrate strength and courage;

   the work that makes all grow and flourish.

   And now this candlelight's display

   will be to honor you this sacred day.

6. Completion: Release layers, deities, and quadrants, and open circle.
7. Ground yourself.

To create an esbat ceremony, refer to the phases of the moon and the names of the new moons (page 52–54). On the night of the full moon (or the night immediately preceding or following it, if that is not possible), plan a celebration to honor the moon and the Goddess. Item 49 shows a sample of an esbat for the Cold Moon or the February full moon.

Item 49. Sample Esbat Ceremony

Purpose: An example for designing an esbat ritual.

1. Prepare your materials and altar.
2. State intention (light working candle).

It is I, [state common or magickal name], *who comes before thee to initiate this circle of power for the purpose I state: Tonight I celebrate the esbat festival of the Cold Moon. I come to honor the Goddess and this time of the year when it is cold and dark, for cold and dark must be celebrated as well as light and warmth. That is my intention.*

3. Banish and purify.
4. Cast the circle.
5. Ritual.
    a. Read the Call of the Goddess aloud.
    b. Enter your inner temple and begin a meditation (see page 137 for how to create your inner temple). Observe the snow melting in your cauldron or chalice. Let those thoughts of cold and hardness melt with the snow. Gather the strength you need to get you through the remaining winter.
    c. When you are through, read aloud the following honor to the Goddess, then light a silver candle.

        O great moon, Goddess entity, the source of femininity, hear my words addressed to thee. I come before thee most reverently. In you I celebrate the receiving; to accept what is true and nurturing. In you I celebrate gentle intuition; the will to trust the unclear vision. And now I this candle light to honor you this sacred night.

6. Completion: Release layers, deities, and quadrants, and open circle.
7. Ground yourself.

Finally, the astor ceremony should be performed near or on the night of the dark moon when the stars are visible. Refer to the qualities of the Child (page 45) and create a ritual that is meaningful to you and a celebration of the mystery of life, which the Child represents. Item 50 shows an example of an astor ceremony.

Item 50. Sample Astor Ritual

Purpose: An example for designing an astor ritual.

1. Prepare materials and altar.
2. State intention (light working candle).

    It is I, [state common or magickal name], *who comes before thee to initiate this circle of power for the purpose I state:*

    Tonight I celebrate the astor and honor the Child. That is my intention.

3. Banish and purify.
4. Cast the circle.
5. Ritual.

    a. Read the Call of the Child aloud.

    b. Enter your inner temple and begin a meditation. Observe those things that are a mystery in your life. Also take a moment to celebrate the fact that you are alive. Think upon those things that bring joy into your life.

    c. When you are through, read aloud the following honor to the Child, then light a black candle.

    O child star, mysterious entity, the source and subject of creativity, hear my words addressed to thee. I come before thee most reverently. In you I celebrate the unbegun; the good work yet to be done. In you I celebrate the great return; the unity of love we have yet to learn. And now I this candle light to honor you this sacred night.

6. Completion: Release layers, deities, and quadrants, and open circle.
7. Ground yourself.

Create Second Degree Magick Books

Now that you have reviewed your Seeker Journal, close it out and begin a new one. This will be your Practitioner Journal and, as before, you should use it whenever you have personal notes about any of your practices. Maintain your daily ritual of writing in your journal.

By now, you should have an extensive set of notes in your Book of Whimsy. It's time to collect and revise these notes into another book— your first Book of Shadows (BoS). You may still want to keep this book in a three-ring binder, but there should be fewer changes to it. Create a fine work of literature for yourself that you can be proud of and which represents your beliefs and traditions. Use magickal alphabets and symbols, for this book is truly yours to treasure. Your BoS might include at least the following: a table of contents, the basic tenets and ethics of your chosen tradition, guidelines for rituals and magick, a description of your ritual tools and objects, specific instructions for magickal work (including some rituals), a listing of levels and degrees of study, a section on your chosen study of divination, a section on your chosen study of healing, a listing of chosen deities or myths, a glossary of terms, and a bibliography.

Create an Inner Temple

You have already created a physical altar that is, in a sense, a temple to your practice. As a budding magician and Priest or Priestess, it becomes more important to work on your level of imagination and visualization. You can create an inner temple that adds to or augments your physical temple. Allow yourself to imagine and create this temple in your mind. Explore different possibilities. What would it look like? What would it be constructed of? What would be inside it? How big would it be? How would it reflect you, your beliefs, your practices? Practice developing this temple in your meditations and using it in your rituals.

Item 51. Ritual for Creating an Inner Temple

Purpose: Create a sacred place in your mind for ritual work.

1. Prepare your space and yourself.
2. State your intention and light a white candle (or brown for building).
3. Banish and purify your space.
4. Cast a circle.
5. Set the four quadrants.
6. Invoke your deities.
7. Call the layers.
8. Begin the ritual.

    a. Begin a meditation and guide yourself to a special place.

    b. Create a sacred area and environment.

    c. Bless and purify the area.

    d. Create a magickal circle.

    e. Build your temple piece by piece.

    f. Enter your temple and consecrate it.

9. End the ritual and open your circle in reverse order.

10. Ground yourself.

When you are ready to begin your building ritual, start by getting comfortable and entering into your meditative state of mind. Remind yourself of your intent—to create a special place in your mind: your inner temple. Begin by finding a clear and open environment in your mind in which to build your special sanctuary. It may be an open field, a mountaintop, a place by the sea, or a place no one else has ever imagined. Look around at the new environment and take it all in. Look in all directions and take careful note of what you see. Get to know this spot of land in your mind. Take in its sights, sounds, smells, topography, and weather. All of these things are under your control.

Now, in your mind, stand in the spot on which you wish to build your temple and state your intention to the environment you created. Just as you did with your physical altar, purify the space upon which your temple shall be constructed. Then, cast a circle in that space. Make sure it is big enough to surround your future temple. Pay homage to the four quadrants, invoke the help of your deities, and set the two layers. Doing these things will create a protective sphere around your temple. Imagine that you have created a magickal bubble that will let your energy out, if you so direct it, but will not allow any unwanted energy in. You are now ready to begin building.

First, decide what material the temple will be made of. It can be constructed of standard building materials, such as wood, stone, or brick. But remember, this is your special temple and it can be made of whatever material you wish—no matter how unusual. Your magickal temple could be built completely out of ice cream if you wish. If you are having trouble seeing the type of building you want, try looking at fantasy books or movies. The first Superman movie, for example, has a scene where Superman builds a crystal temple in the Arctic. There are many other examples available if you look around. You might also think back to your childhood. Were there any buildings or places that were special to you? Did you build forts or tree houses? What did you dream they were made of?

Once you have your material in mind, begin constructing the outside walls. They need not be square or even completely solid. Let them take on whatever shape you wish. Decide if you want extra floors or just one flat space. When the walls are finished, add a door and some windows if you wish. Enter your temple and look at the bare walls and floors inside. You may wish to add items to the insides of the walls. Does it need torches, candles, or colored lights? What about a ritual item or tool on each wall that represents the four quarters? Do you wish to add items that represent your deities? Look at the floor. How do you want it decorated? Shall it honor Mother Earth? Look up. What is above you? Shall it honor Father Sky? Look toward the center of the room and start to build your special altar. It may look like your physical altar or it could be completely different. You may want it to be just a simple pedestal upon which different items and tools will be placed according to the type of work that will be done. You decide.

When you are completely through building your temple, step back and take a good look at it. Remember all its details so you can easily return to it when you need it. If everything is as you would like it, consecrate your sacred inner temple, then leave and return to the physical world. Remember to ground yourself when you are through. The next time you work with your inner temple, send a call out to the universe that you wish to contact the presence of the mysterious. Then, allow it to happen. If it does not happen at first, be patient and try another time.

Enact Special Meditations

A major part of the work of this degree will be to practice a variety of meditations. By now, you should have established a regular practice time and ritual for meditation. If you have not, you should consider doing so. It will be much easier to remember to practice if a regular schedule is created and maintained. By now you should also have developed a routine for regular ritual practice that includes a standard opening and closing for starting a ritual, blessing your space, creating a circle, and reversing the procedure to end. This regular routine will become an important part of developing specialized meditations and rituals. As always, if you feel it is necessary to make changes, then do so, because creativity is as equally important as routine. It is much more important to approach your rituals with a sense of freshness and joyousness rather than maintaining the same stale routine. With your inner temple created, you now have a place in your mind to go to do your work.

The Seven Main Chakras

An important part of spiritual development is the opening of the chakras. You learned about the chakras in the first degree, as well as the many things with which each is associated (page 105). It is believed that each chakra center is a connection of the energies between the physical body and the higher bodies that exist simultaneously with the physical body but on higher planes. By "opening up" each of the chakras, the energy flow between the bodies is established or increased, which leads to better health and the development of psychic abilities. There are many systems designed to do this work. No one system is better or more correct than another. One system involves using the sounds and colors of each chakra. While meditating, concentrate on the qualities attached to the chakra, focus on that part of the body, see it as emanating the associated color, and hum softly (or internally) the sound to which it is associated. Remember that each meditation should continue for a minimum time of 20 minutes. Half an hour to an hour would be better, but practicality may demand shorter periods.

For each meditation, light a candle that is the same color as the related chakra, and then create your ritual space and circle as you have designed in your normal ritual process. Enter your inner temple and begin creating a meditative frame of mind. Focus your attention on the related part of the body. While breathing in, concentrate on bringing up earth energy into your body, and then let it circulate in that body area as you breathe out. Each chakra also has an additional point of focus, depending on the quality of that chakra. After you have settled into a routine of focused breathing, allow your mind to concentrate on the focus of that particular chakra. Item 52 shows a chart listing the centers of focus for each chakra.

Item 52. Chakra Meditation

Purpose: Methods of focus to open each chakra.

First Chakra

Candle Color:	red
Area of Body:	base of spine
Sound:	hmm (C)
Focus:	deep relaxation

Second Chakra

Candle Color:	orange
Area of Body:	genitals
Sound:	hee (D)
Focus:	emotional relaxation

Third Chakra

Candle Color:	yellow
Area of Body:	navel
Sound:	heh (E)
Focus:	one-pointed mind

Fourth Chakra

Candle Color:	green
Area of Body:	heart
Sound:	huh (F)
Focus:	loving kindness

Fifth Chakra

Candle Color:	blue
Area of Body:	throat
Sound:	hoh (G)
Focus:	deep listening

Sixth Chakra

Candle Color:	purple
Area of Body:	third eye
Sound:	hah (A)
Focus:	visualization

Seventh Chakra

Candle Color:	white
Area of Body:	crown
Sound:	aum (B)
Focus:	absorption

An example of how to use the previous chart is to begin with the first chakra for a series of meditations. Light a red candle while stating your intent. Close your circle and begin your meditation. Concentrate on circulating energy at the base of your spine. Audibly or inwardly make a "hmm" sound. If you wish, you can use the note C as your pitch for humming. As you continue to hum, concentrate on making your body deeply and completely relaxed. Try to maintain this meditation for at least 20 minutes, then open your circle and complete your ritual.

For the second chakra, light an orange candle, concentrate on the area around your genitals (you may even become sexually aroused—use this powerful energy in your body), make the sound "hee" (on the note D), and concentrate on relaxing your emotional self. To do this, learn to accept yourself for just who you are. Realize that you are a developing being and that is part of your life's goal. Accept your imperfections and celebrate your strengths. Believe in who you are because there is no one quite like you in the entire world.

The theme of the third chakra is to develop the ability to focus your willpower. Light a yellow candle, concentrate on the center of the body around the navel, and hum "heh" (on the note E). Concentrate on the one-pointed mind. That is the mind of complete concentration. Focus all your thoughts entirely on the "heh" sound you are making. Let no other thoughts invade your mind. If they do, do not chastise yourself. Simply bring your mind back to the focus and begin again.

For the fourth chakra, light a green candle and concentrate on the loving feelings surrounding the heart. Tone on the "huh" syllable (on the note F). Feel a sense of loving kindness. Similar to the ongoing practice for this degree, focus on how you can feel a sense of acceptance and love for all creatures.

With the fifth chakra, use a blue candle. Concentrate on how you communicate by thinking about the throat area. Make a "hoh" sound (on the note G). Develop a sense of deep listening. Focus your listening inward and be prepared to hear messages from deep within. If you hear nothing, this is fine, because you may not need to receive any messages at this time.

For the sixth chakra, light a purple candle while concentrating on the psychic area of the third eye—in the middle of your forehead. Use a "hah" sound (on the note A). Develop your powers of inner visualization. Visualize an object and hold it in your mind as long as possible. Let your imagination alter the object in different ways if you wish. The important thing is to keep the image in your mind as long as possible.

For the seventh chakra, focus of concentration will probably be the most difficult. Use a white candle and focus on the top of your head—your crown. Make an "aum" sound (on the note B). The aum is a complex sound unlike the simple sounds of the earlier chakras. The three letters A-U-M each have a distinct sound and you should say the word slowly and deliberately so that each sound is heard. The type of focus needed for this chakra is called absorption. The method is to take an object, such as a candle (or for a very advanced meditation, a deity), and concentrate on it. The goal is to concentrate on the object (or idea) to such a degree that you and the object no longer exist as separate beings. Try to lose your sense of self and become the object you are focusing upon. Try to see what it is like to be that object. What does it and you have in common? Find the true essence that is a part of you and it. Try to hold onto this feeling as long as possible.

In each of these meditations, allow any feelings of a presence beyond yourself to come into your thoughts and sensations. Explore what this presence may be. Be sure to record the results of all your practices into your Practitioner Journal.

Elemental Meditations

The next set of meditations is devised to help the practitioner connect with the four elements of Wiccan practice (the fifth will come later). Review the chart you entered in your BoS related to the four elements. Read over the qualities of each element. For each, devise a way in which you can connect with that element through your meditation. For example, an Air meditation may be done in a high place where you feel a connection to the air. A Fire meditation may be done near a campfire or woodstove. A Water meditation may be done near a body of water or with a ritual bath, and an Earth meditation may be done outside in a grove of trees.

For each meditation, study the correspondences of the element and what each is related to in your life and practice. Most of these meditations are best done outdoors with the elements themselves. Remember to purify and bless the space on which you meditate. Close your circle and quarters with appropriate markers or stones and, as always, ground yourself when you are through.

The following chart relates each of the elements to a color, a representative item, a place or natural item related to that element, a focus for your meditation, and the related direction of each element.

Item 53. Elemental Meditations

Purpose: Suggestions to enact elemental meditations.

Element	Color	Item	Place	Focus	Direction
Earth	green	salt	woods, open land	grounding	North
Air	yellow	athame	high overlook	pure thoughts	East
Fire	red	wand	fireplace, bonfire	relationships	South
Water	blue	cup	body of water	inner feelings	West

To apply this information to making meaningful meditations on the elements, choose an element with which to begin your first meditation. The time of year and your particular location might determine which element should be first. Fire is a good element to meditate upon in the Winter, especially if you have a fireplace. Taking a ritual bath can be a powerful Water meditation and can be done when the weather is unfriendly. Earth and Air, however, might be elements with which a connection might be more powerful if you are outdoors. Taking a look at each element, we will see how each can be used as a focus for meditation.

Earth Meditation

An Earth meditation might best be done outdoors. A private place in the woods or a special clearing can help you to feel directly connected with the earth. Take with you a green stone or candle and some salt or an herb. After performing your basic ritual routine, sit facing the direction of North, place your stone or candle in front of you, as well as your salt or herb. Light the candle, stating your intention, or hold the stone close to you and concentrate on your intention and then place the stone before you. Look at the salt or herb (you may wish to spread it about you) and take a few minutes to think about the element of Earth and all its manifestations in your life and the world around you. Then, begin your meditation concentrating either upon your thoughts about the element of Earth or upon grounding yourself with the earth. Feel as if you are a part of the earth as a plant might feel with its roots deeply clinging to the soil. Some like to do the Earth meditation with a tree because the tree is an important part of the earth but also because the tree is a symbol of the connections between below (with its roots) and above (with its branches).

Air Meditation

The Air meditation is best done outdoors in a high location or a place in which you can feel the force of the air blowing on you. Take a yellow candle or stone with you, as well as your athame or other symbol of Air. Follow the same process as with Earth, but facing East. Meditate on the meaning of Air and how this element manifests itself in the world, or concentrate on having pure thoughts—that is to say, thoughts of high ideals, purity, and clarity. This, of course, is a very difficult task but worth the effort.

Fire Meditation

Fire is best experienced in the safe presence of a controlled fire such as in a fireplace, campfire, or bonfire. Sit where you can safely feel the heat and see the flames of a fire. If a large outdoor fire is not available, use a red candle or stone. Bring your wand to your meditation. Face South and meditate upon Fire itself or upon the way that the many different people in your life act and interact with you. Observe the myriad connections of people and the web of life of which you are an important part.

Water Meditation

For a meditation on Water, consider being near a body of water. Sitting by the side of a pond or stream, sitting in a boat on a lake, sitting near a waterfall, or just sitting in the midst of a warm pouring rain can be some of the many ways in which Water can be experienced during a meditation. Use a blue candle or stone and bring your chalice or other symbol of Water. Concentrate on the meaning of Water to you or meditate on your inner feelings—that flowing substance within you that is constantly changing. Observe your true inner feelings and what brings about their existence. Ask yourself how these feelings come about, how they affect your life, why they sometimes conflict with what you express outwardly, and how they affect the people around you.

These are just some suggestions for ways to connect with the elements. The important thing is to find a way that resonates with you and makes for a meaningful and joyous connection with these powerful parts of our world. It is also possible to combine one or more of these meditations together. One of my most memorable meditations was done on top of a waterfall. I felt the water rush around me and I felt the air blow gently on my face. I felt the heat of the fire of the sun and I felt below me the huge rock that made up the cliffs of the waterfall.

The Three Deities

Similar to the elemental meditations, further meditations should be enacted on the three deities. These can be on the general principles of each or on specific deities if they have been chosen. Study the correspondences and characteristics of each deity and how they are related to your life and practice. Remember that, unlike other religions, these gods are not angry, jealous rulers for whom you must relegate your life. Instead, these energies are to serve you for right and good. Worship and study them to further your practice and to better yourself and others.

You may wish to choose specific traditional deities, or you may wish to concentrate on deities as representations of cosmic forces. Either way, come to understand the qualities of each by meditating on them. Then, engage in a ritual in which you aspect these deities by calling on them for guidance. For each meditation, find a spot outside or inside where you will not be disturbed. Purify the space and set your circle. Invoke the deity and ask for his or her guidance and protection. Then begin a meditation where you focus on drawing the presence of that deity and its characteristics into your life.

As before, we will begin with a chart of information that you may refer to for the design of your meditations.

Item 54. Meditations on the Three Deities

Purpose: Suggestions for ways to meditate and aspect the gods.

God

Candle color:	gold, yellow
Planet:	the sun
Object:	athame, wand
Time:	before the light of dawn
Location:	an outside place to view the sunrise
Focus:	strength and light

Goddess

Candle color:	silver, white
Planet:	the moon
Object:	chalice and stone, salt
Time:	in the evening during the night of a full moon
Location:	outside in view of the full moon
Focus:	compassion and love

Child

Candle color: black, purple
Planet: the stars
Object: plants, herbs
Time: in the evening during a dark moon
Location: outside in view of the stars
Focus: silence and the gift of life

Because these meditations are about deities and not specific elements, they can be done anywhere. However, as Pagans, we often use the sun, moon, and stars as symbols or representations of these deities. A meditation on the concept of the God may be done outside where the sun can be felt directly. One of the most powerful times of the day for meditation, especially one that includes the sun, is dawn. Many traditions believe that dawn is a time of great strength. Consider doing a meditation that includes watching the sunrise. As you watch the dawn unfold before you, consider what the male deity or qualities of the masculine means to you and your life. How does the sun play an important role to you and all life around you? What does the heat and light of the sun symbolize to you? Consider how the sun symbolizes strength and growth and how those qualities can be important to you. Take along a yellow or gold candle and an item that represents to you maleness or masculinity. You may consider saying an invocation such as: "God of the Sun, great masculine one, let your work through me be done. Protect and guide me all these days as I come to learn your ways."

Meditations for the Goddess and the Child might best be done at night. Find a place where you can clearly observe the light of the moon for the Goddess meditation. Bring along a silver or white candle or stone, and an object that represents to you qualities of the feminine. As you observe the moon, consider how femininity plays an important part in you and your life. (Remember that all things have qualities of the masculine and the feminine.) What does the moon and its light symbolize to you? How can you better incorporate the softer qualities of love and compassion in your life and within your relationships with others? Consider saying an invocation such as: "Goddess of the Moon, great feminine one, let your work through me be done. Protect and guide me through the nights as I come to learn your rites."

The Child meditation is also best done at night, but when there appears to be no moon so that the stars can be seen easily. Find a place outside where you can easily view the many stars overhead. Though they may be no more than billions of suns much like our own sun, they are, to us, tiny beacons of light that pierce the darkness just as each of us are tiny vessels of light. Small lights in the darkness are a symbol of hope, and each person that feels the joy of life within is a person of hope. This is what the Child represents—the myriad lights sparkling against the darkness that is life. Use a black or purple candle or stone and a symbol of life as you begin your meditation. Concentrate on what life means to you. Do you live your life as someone who respects the gifts of the light of the God and the love of the Goddess? How can you be a being of hope rather than despair? How can you learn to appreciate the darkness and the silence as equally important components of your life? Consider the following invocation or create one of your own: "Child of the stars, great mysterious one, let your work through me be done. Protect and guide me through the years as divine wisdom to me appears."

Symbolic Meditations

In the first degree, you began a study of methods of divination. Many of those methods, including tarot cards and runes, use a series of symbols to represent deeper meanings. Choose a symbolic sequence, such as the major arcana of the tarot cards, and engage in a meditation ritual for each card. It is best to create your own meanings from the symbols, but if this is difficult, read the guidebook that came with your cards or other tools and use the suggested meanings for each symbol. Create a checklist to mark your progress. Determine what each means to you and your practice. Set out a list of each of the items and write out their meanings. This can be done as daily meditations. You can take the next item in the sequence (or you can choose randomly) and concentrate on its meaning in a short morning meditation. Then, apply the meaning of that item toward the day's activities. For example, if you were to choose the tarot card marked The Magician, you might observe how the ability to change things might be applied to your life's activities. Some methods of ritual meditation can also be done with the Hebrew alphabet, astrological signs, the Chinese horoscope, the runes, the I Ching, animal representations, colors, tree representations, or numbers, just to name a few. Choose whatever system appeals to you. The chart in Item 55 uses the major arcana of the tarot cards as an example.

Item 55. Major Arcana Cards as Meditations

Purpose: Give examples of a focus for symbolic meditations.

Number	Card	Question
0	Fool	How can I be open to new beginnings?
1	Magus	What is the role of the God in daily life?
2	Priestess	What is the role of the Goddess in daily life?
3	Empress	What is the role of the mother?
4	Emperor	What is the role of the father?
5	Hierophant	How can I make a change for the better?
6	Lovers	How can I learn to be more loving?
7	Chariot	What is my direction?
8	Adjustment	How can justice be sought in relationships?
9	Hermit	When is silence needed more often?
10	Fortune	What is the role of change?
11	Lust	What desires are necessary/unnecessary?
12	Hanged Man	What can I sacrifice for greater good?
13	Death	What do I need to end or bring back to life?
14	Art	How does creativity play a role in my life?
15	Devil	How can I regain a sense of joy and fun?
16	Tower	What is holding me back from progress in life?
17	Star	What do I hope for? Is it worthwhile and realistic?
18	Moon	How can I nurture my feminine side?
19	Sun	How can I foster my masculine side?
20	Aeon	Where do I need to apply patience and understanding?
21	Universe	Where do I need to find wholeness and unity in my life?

Raise and Direct Energy

An important aspect of spellcasting and healing is the raising and direction of energy. Study modern physics to understand the principles behind the force of energy alive in all of us. Then, study and practice in order to learn to awaken and use this energy. There are many ways of raising energy within yourself. Some of the most popular are through chanting or just concentrating on moving energy. Some people use movements. You may want to look into movement methods such as t'ai chi, yoga, and chi kung. Enact a ritual using your inner temple to raise and direct this energy. Be sure to clearly set your goals for this action. Check to make sure that what you are doing is ethically sound and be sure to protect yourself and ground yourself afterward. Here is an example of a ritual for raising energy.

Item 56. Ritual for Raising Energy

Purpose: An example of a ritual that can be used for raising energy that can be directed for magickal or healing needs.

1. Prepare your space and yourself.
2. State your intention and light a pink candle (for loving energy).
3. Banish and purify your space.
4. Cast a circle.
5. Enter your inner temple.
6. Begin the ritual.
   - Focus on someone whom you think might need loving energy.
   - Begin a soft hum either audibly or internally.
   - Set your arms down to your sides.
   - Imagine filling your body with feelings of pure unconditional love.
   - You may imagine filling yourself with a pink, white, or clear light.
   - See that energy filling the lower part of your body where your hands now rest.
   - Continue to hum and very slowly raise your arms.

+ You may want to hum louder or raise the pitch as you go.
+ See the light filling your body as you raise your arms.
+ Also see your inner temple filling up with this light.
+ Let it swirl about you like a tornado with a cone of power that slowly rises above your temple.
+ Let your hands continue upward until they are nearly together over your head.
+ When you and your temple are completely full of energy, clap your hands once briskly.
+ Imagine releasing that energy through yourself and upward through your temple.
+ Visualize directing that energy toward the person you chose.
+ See that person becoming filled with your warm and loving energy.

7. End the ritual, exit your temple, and open your circle in reverse order.
8. Ground yourself.

Develop Methods for Aura Cleansing and Protection

The concept of the aura can be a difficult one, but understanding it is an important tool. As you begin to understand the principles of raising and directing energy, you will realize the importance of keeping the energy around you pure. Similarly, you will begin to sense the ways in which others can direct and manipulate their energy toward you. It is important to begin to learn how to cleanse and protect your own personal space.

If you are like most people, you probably spend a great deal of time around others and, unless you work all day at home, you probably spend a lot of time in places that are not your own or do not have all your own energy. This means that throughout the day, you may be picking up bits of energy from all these people and places. Most of this energy is probably harmless, but some will be connected with those people who are not happy. They may be angry or depressed.

They may harbor thoughts of harm or revenge. Or they may just be people who have never learned to enjoy life and, so, carry with them these feelings of sadness and uneasiness. Thus, you may be unknowingly collecting some of this energy, which may become attached to your aura. At the end of the day, it may help to take some time to clear your personal space free of this undesired energy.

Item 57. Activity for Cleansing Aura

Purpose: Clear unwanted energies.

- Stand in a quiet and clear space.
- Clear your mind.
- Extend your arms forward.
- Concentrate on raising a small amount of energy.
- Circle around clockwise to create a magick circle around yourself.
- Face each quarter separately and bow or acknowledge each as you go.
- Invoke your deities and set the layers to create a protective sphere around you.
- Stand comfortably with hands together in front of you (prayer position) and concentrate on creating a white light above you.
- Let the white light slowly fill your space (aura), moving slowly downward.
- As it moves and fills your space, feel it collecting all unwanted energies.
- Let the light drain down below your feet into the ground.
- Take a minute to enjoy the refreshed feeling of being cleared.
- Open your circle and ground yourself.

You can also do something to protect yourself from picking up any unwanted energies. There may be times when someone is consciously directing negative energies toward you. Anytime that someone is angry at you or expresses the desire to cause you harm or discomfort, there is an intent behind that desire and that intent is filled with energy. The person may not even be aware of this use of energy but it is there nonetheless. It is important to learn how to protect yourself from these types of psychic attacks. Learn to use your aura as a shield.

Item 58. Creating a Protective Shield

Purpose: For protection against directed negative energy.

- Stand in a quiet and clear space.
- Clear your mind.
- Extend your arms forward.
- Concentrate on raising a small amount of energy.
- Circle around clockwise to create a magick circle around yourself.
- Face each quarter separately and bow or acknowledge each as you go.
- Invoke your deities and set the layers to create a protective sphere around you.
- Stand in a meditative posture and concentrate on creating a strong red light from within.
- Let the red light slowly fill your space (aura), moving slowly outward.
- As it moves and fills your space, feel it creating a protective barrier.
- See the red light take on the shape of a protective bubble around you.
- Take a moment to enjoy this protective feeling.
- Open your circle and ground yourself.
- If you need to use it, fill up your aura quickly with this red light and hold it there.

Begin Psychic Work

Psychic ability is being able to perceive beyond the normal level of the senses. This information can be used to help yourself and others.

To develop psychic ability, you have to learn how to tune into your normal senses and heighten them. For example, clairvoyance and being able to see the aura are developed through heightened seeing, clairaudience is heightened hearing, and psychometry is heightened touch.

Wiccans believe that every person has some level of psychic ability and that such an ability can be developed and strengthened in every person. This does not mean that everyone can become an instant psychic. Some have more natural talent than others, but everyone has some degree of ability. Almost everyone has experienced some tinge of psychic connection. Thinking of someone when, suddenly, the phone rings and that person's voice is on the other end, suddenly turning around because you have the feeling that someone else is watching you from behind, or knowing what someone is about to say before it is said are all examples of common occurrences of psychic ability. This ability can be developed and strengthened with practice. If you find, however, that you have difficulty developing any of these senses, do not be discouraged. Just knowing how to develop these abilities may be enough for you to help someone else. There is something in the Craft for everyone to develop their talents.

Item 59. Methods of Psychic Ability

Purpose: Notice different methods to practice and study.

aura sensing:	Seeing and reading the energy field of living beings.
automatic writing:	Free writing with no conscious goal.
clairvoyance:	Heightened seeing.
clairaudience:	Heightened hearing.
divination:	Using tools of chance to gain information (for more information, see methods of divination on pages 109–111).
dream work:	Interpreting images and messages from dreams.
necromancy:	Gaining information from spirits of different realms.
psychometry:	Heightened touch.

scrying or	
crystal gazing:	Using an object as a focus for seeing images.
telepathy:	Gaining impressions or thoughts from other people.

There are many different ways in which psychic ability can be developed and manifested. I will offer several ways in this book in a sequence. You may work in this sequence or develop your own. If you find an area in which you develop greater interest or a natural ability, then spend extra time developing that specialty. Be sure to record the results of all your work into your journal.

First Steps of Psychic Work

The first step in developing psychic ability is to simply accept those parts of you that are already open to psychic awareness. This means not denying those strange feelings and sensations you have had all your life. In our Western culture, we are taught to ignore and dismiss any unexplainable feelings, sensations, or hunches. It is time to reverse that attitude and respect, honor, and, more importantly, pay attention to any of those sensations. Take notice when your feelings or mood changes suddenly in a room full of people. Take notice when you feel you know something just as it is about to happen. Take notice when you hear unusual sounds or voices, feel strange feelings, or see unexplainable images. The appearance of these things does not necessarily mean that you are going crazy. Honor these feelings! They may be signals, warnings, or just important pieces of information for you. Stop dismissing these things; pay attention to them. You do not have to understand any of them for now—that will come eventually. For now, just pay attention. These may be calls to you from something greater.

Meditation Practices

You have already started on the road to psychic development by developing and maintaining a regular practice of meditation. Apply your concentration to gazing at something, such as a candle flame or an item from your altar. Try to see beyond the object. Observe not just the thing itself, but its essence. After you have tried careful observation, try to visualize that object in your mind. See it as intensely as if your eyes were still open and you were staring at that object as before. Move the object around in your mind. Next, engage your sense of touch by feeling the object. Be sure to observe all the sensations you feel as you engage it. Let the object roll in your hands. Feel how the texture changes. For your next meditation, visualize the object as before, but, this time, imagine touching and holding the object in your mind. These are just a few of the things that you can do in your meditation practice to increase your sense of awareness, which is a first step in psychic development.

Psychometry

The next thing you may wish to try and develop is a heightened sense of touch through the practice of psychometry. Psychometry is the ability to sense energies that are stored in objects. All of us are bundles of constantly moving energy and some of this energy leaves our presence and can be stored in other objects or, sometimes, people. It is possible to detect these energies and then get an idea of what may have previously come in contact with certain objects.

The first step for honing this capability is to develop the sensitivity in your fingertips. Do this by gently rubbing your fingertips together. There should be a slight tingling feeling. With your fingers still tingling, find an object to touch. Apply only the slightest amount of pressure so that your fingertips barely connect with the object. Slowly pull the object away and see how far you can move from it while still feeling a sensation of the object in your fingers. Try to get to the point where you can still sense the object even though it no longer is in contact with your fingers. Do this with several different objects of varying textures. As you do this practice, open your mind and enter your meditative state. Try to detect any impressions, thoughts, or images you might get while feeling the object. Be open to anything you might receive. Do the same practice with the palms of your hands. Gently rub them together until they tingle and begin the process of putting objects in your palms. Again, notice any feelings or sensations you might receive, then slowly remove the object.

At first, do this practice with objects that you have owned yourself and notice if you can detect your own energies. After several practice sessions, start using objects that others have owned, or, if possible, objects whose owner is unfamiliar to you. Notice if your mood or train of thought changes. Notice any changes in your body. Observe any images or impressions that come into your mind. Another interesting experiment is to take a set of objects, such as very similar car keys that belong to other people, and mix them up. Feel each object as you have done in your exercises and try to determine who the owner of the object is without looking at the object. Observe the impressions you get from touching the object and see if they remind you of one of the owners.

Viewing Auras

A good way of developing a heightened visual sense is to practice developing the ability to see energy auras. Auras are fields of energy that surround living beings. (Some even say that there are auras around all objects.) The ability to see auras leads to increased understanding of people's expressions and can aid in the process of psychic healing.

To develop the detection of auras, you may want to begin by sitting and observing a crystal or a magnet in a dimly lit room. Crystals and magnets both naturally possess energy waves within and around them. It takes a great deal of time and patience to begin to see an aura, so it helps to begin with an object that, hopefully, will not oppose your staring at it for a long period of time. As you look at the object, relax your body and mind as much as possible. Do not look directly at the object in focus. Instead, look beyond the object. Let your eyes become unfocused. Imagine that you are not looking at it with just your two eyes. Use the concept of the "third eye"—the place in the middle of your forehead where your sixth chakra resides. Imagine that you can see with this eye as well, but not as your other two eyes can see. The third eye psychically sees beyond the object. Take your time and allow this sense to develop slowly. At first, you may see nothing, then you may get a glimpse of something—the excitement of which may cause you to loose your concentration. Try to remain focused on your goal and not the results until the ability slowly develops.

The next step in development would be to put a dark background behind the same object and a moderately bright light behind you, pointing towards the object. Begin to see the object in the same manner as before, but this time with the added light. Be patient and see through the object. Then, do the same thing with a living flower (do not use a cut flower). Put a dark background behind the flower and a light behind you that shines upon the flower. Let yourself begin the process of observing the plant's aura. Take notice of any changes in the shapes around the plant. Do you see any colors? Do they change? Send loving energy to the plant. Does its aura change when you do that? Do the same process to a plant or tree outside. Unfocus your eyes and concentrate on seeing its aura. Remember to take your time and be patient with yourself.

If you have been successful with these exercises, then it is time to develop the ability with people. You can begin with yourself. Cup your hands as if you were holding a ball in each hand. Without touching, point your fingertips toward the fingertips of your other hand. With a white background behind your hands, look at the space between your fingertips. See if you can observe any movement. At first, you may see clear ripples similar to the ripples you see on dark pavement when it is very hot outside. These ripples may then change from clear to lines filled with color. When you have developed this capability, do the same process with another person. It is best if you observe someone for a long period of time who has a solid background behind him or her. It may be difficult to convince a friend to stand against a white wall for a long time. Instead, go to an event that will have a speaker. If you can find a good place to observe the speaker, you will be able to study the aura of this person for quite some time without being accused of rude staring. If, after this point, you have found it easy to read auras, you can then practice seeing them on any person in any situation.

Scrying

Scrying is an ancient practice of inner seeing. By looking deeply into an object, it is possible to get impressions and images that may provide useful information to the seer. One of the most well-known objects in the practice of scrying is the crystal ball, but other objects can be used as well. Some use a black mirror or a darkened bowl filled with water. Some use very simple objects, such as a plain glass of water or a crystal. Use whatever feels most useful to you.

The process for scrying is fairly simple. Find an object you wish to use, such as the ones previously mentioned. Enter your meditative state. Look into the object, not at the object. Look beyond it and let your eyes relax. As before, use the ability of your third eye. At some point, you should begin to see the object clouding up. Continue to relax and wait until the clouds either begin to form images or dissipate, leaving impressions and images. Take careful note of what you see and how you feel.

Dream Work

One of the most powerful methods for developing psychic ability is through an occurrence that happens every night—the dreams you have in your sleep. Much information can be learned from the images that appear to you while you sleep. The trick is in interpreting these images. There are many good books available that describe common images and symbols and what they mean. However, it is best to try and discern the meanings for yourself. Images can mean many different things to different people, and the images you see will be meaningful according to your own experience and learning.

The trick to doing dream work is to find ways for your conscious mind to access the dreams that take place in your unconscious mind. There are several ways to do this. You can try to drift off to sleep slowly. When you are aware that you are in that state between waking and sleeping, try to coax your conscious mind into staying alert as you begin to drift off to sleep. You may be able to be aware of some images before you actually fall completely asleep. But the best time to recall images is just before you begin to really awaken. It is quite useful to keep your Seeker Journal by your bedside so that you can jot down your impressions before you are fully awake and your memories of the previous night's dreams are erased. Some people even keep a separate dream journal. Another useful method is to encourage yourself to remember your dreams just before you go to sleep. You may infuse your desire and energy into a crystal or a dream pillow with a special ritual. Before going to sleep, hold the crystal or pillow in your hand and re-infuse the object with your energy and desire. Place the object under your pillow and go to sleep while concentrating on your goal.

Often, what makes it difficult for us to remember our dreams in the morning is the disruptive way in which we wake ourselves. A sudden sound, such as that created by an alarm clock, awakens us with a quick surprise. Finding a way to more gently wake yourself encourages your mind to wake up slowly and gently. A slower transition from dreaming to waking can help the conscious mind to remember unconscious images. Try finding an alarm that slowly and gently awakens you. Set it earlier so that you still wake at the same time, but, instead, are gradually brought out of sleep. Make sure you take note of any images you may remember.

Clairvoyance and Clairaudience

Both heightened seeing and heightened hearing are best developed from meditative practices. Begin with the visualization practices described on pages 156–157. Develop the ability to see and manipulate an object in your mind. Try to see all the details of the object clearly in your mind. Next, with your eyes open, clearly observe an object in a particular environment away from where you usually meditate. Observe the details of the object, but also clearly observe the details of the environment. Notice every shape, color, and texture. Memorize the details. During your next meditation session, imagine that you have a small screen in your mind much like a television set. See in your mind the same scene that you observed before. Again, recall all the details as clearly as you can. Now, concentrate on actually seeing that scene, not just your memory of it. Imagine that your small mental screen is actually a screen that allows you to view the place as it currently exists—as if you had a camera placed in that location and you were watching the monitor. Has the scene changed at all? Try to view different scenes on subsequent sessions. Try also to see images of people you know on your psychic screen. Notice where they are and what they are doing. Confirm your observations by calling them up afterward and asking what they were doing.

To develop heightened hearing, begin by listening deeply to your own body during your meditation sessions. Hear every part of your body at work as you sit. Next, return to the place where you practiced careful observation. This time, close your eyes and carefully listen to every sound you hear. Identify all the separate sounds and then relax and listen to all of them together as they combine into one beautiful, natural symphony. Return to your meditative practice and concentrate on hearing all those same sounds in your mind. As you are listening, pay careful attention to any additional noises that may come into your awareness. Are there voices or unusual sounds that may communicate a message to you? You can also practice intense listening. When someone speaks to you, try to listen intently without any additional thoughts in your mind. Pay attention to what the speaker is saying, but also be open to additional words or sounds that may come to you as you are listening.

Telepathy

To develop a sense of telepathy, you will need a willing and understanding partner. It is your goal to try and gain thoughts and impressions from this person, so it must be someone you can trust and who understands what it is you are trying to accomplish. One of the best ways to start development is with the use of a common deck of playing cards. Have your partner shuffle the deck and then pull a random card. Your first goal is to try and determine if the card selected is red or black. Have your partner clear her mind and concentrate on the image on the card. Have her see the color in her own mind and ask her to project that color to you. Relax and enter your meditative state of mind. Do not try to force yourself into getting an answer quickly. Let your mind clear until an image eventually enters your mind. Take careful note as to the percentage of correct and incorrect answers. See if you can increase the percentage with additional practice.

When you feel as though you have a fairly good average of determining the color of the cards, move on to determining the suit. With only red or black as your choices, you only had two possibilities. Concentrating on the suits gives you a choice of four. Use the same method as before. Make sure your partner is concentrating on the image of the suit in her mind while you clear yours and prepare to receive the image of that suit in your mind. After using the four suits, remove the Jacks, Queens, and Kings, and practice reading the 10 numbers (10 choices). Next, remove the Aces and practice reading the suit and name of these cards (16 choices). Finally, put all the cards together and practice seeing the exact card (52 choices).

If you have found some moderate success with the cards, you can then work on developing your ability further. Have your partner think of a simple image and, as before, have her project that image to you. You can further practice by being aware of thoughts, images, and impressions you receive in the presence of others, including plants and animals. Observe your ability to pick up thoughts and impressions from other people. Take special note if your mood or feelings change when certain people pass you by. If you can (without being rude, of course), confirm your impressions by talking to those from whom you received an impression. If you were wrong, do not fret. You may have received the impression from a different person or object. It is also possible that you read something of which the person is not even aware of himself. As always, follow your own ethical principles and intuition in discussing these things with others.

Other Practices

At this level, you should begin teaching and reaching out to others. It is often the teacher that learns more than the student because teaching requires the tutor to organize and clarify concepts. Furthermore, one of the responsibilities of learning the Craft is to pass on this information to any who seek it. Find those who are pursuing the first degree and assist them as you can. You can also practice mentoring by teaching a class or workshop in a local Pagan study group.

Finally, we often forget that the pursuit of spiritual truths requires that we turn away from our own needs and help others. There is a tremendous amount of spiritual development that comes through helping others. Seek out an established group that regularly does community work, and volunteer. Notice the spiritual messages you receive through this work.

Initiation to Second Degree

You have learned a great deal and now it is time to recognize your achievements. First, just as you did with the previous degree, review your progress of what you have accomplished so far.

Once you have completed your review and believe that you are ready to accept the level of second degree, write a second degree Initiation ceremony that is meaningful to you. Be sure to cast a circle and implement the things you have learned about ritual and ceremony. Mark the date of your Initiation, because further study requires a year and a day of work beyond that date.

Congratulations, Mistress or Master! You are now a Wiccan Priest or Priestess! Put a red cord on your pendant and celebrate! You are now ready to begin work on the third degree.

Chapter 4

Che Chird Oegree: Path of the Soul

- ∼ Number: 3
- ∼ Title: Wiccan High Priest or Priestess
- ∼ Prefix: Lady or Lord
- ∼ Color: blue
- ∼ Gift: chalice, cauldron
- ∼ Goals:
    1. Profess a desire to continue the study of the Craft of Wicca.
    2. Pursue the second Great Mystery.
    3. Create third degree books.
    4. Create and enact personal and/or group rituals for all sabbats, esbats, astors, and other ceremonies.
    5. Learn advanced techniques for leading a group in ritual, including theater, music, and drumming.
    6. Enact meditations on the element of Spirit and kundalini raising.
    7. Learn the principles of group building and group dynamics.
    8. Begin your own study group or non-traditional coven.
    9. Learn the principles of advising.

10. Begin an advanced study of magick; learn channeling and gain a spirit familiar.
11. Begin advanced study of healing and divination.
12. Teach others.
13. Write and enact an Initiation to the third degree.

In the second degree, you became a Priest or Priestess, which means that you have the knowledge and experience to be a highly developed spiritual being. But a truly developed spiritual person knows that learning and developing does not end with the self. Most great spiritual leaders knew that they could not just be content with living a spiritual life alone—they became teachers and leaders for others. That is what a High Priest or Priestess is—a spiritual leader for others. Learning and developing does not stop while leading others, though. It continues at a more profound level than before. In the third degree, you may choose to continue developing those skills you began earlier while also learning about how to teach and lead others.

If you have chosen to be a solitary practitioner, then you may decide that the second degree is your final level, so you could choose things from this degree that would relate to your own development. You might also remain solitary but take on individual students in which to engage in these activities. All of this is for you to decide. The goal of this level is to learn to lead others and to experience how all things are connected as one.

The Second Great Mystery

In the pursuit of the second degree, you were asked to seek the answer to the first Great Mystery of what exists beyond ourselves. It is one thing to talk about Spirit, but it is quite another to actually experience it. Hopefully, at some point in the previous year, you were able to do just that—experience a little bit of the Divine. Gaining some small understanding of that experience and its source will give you an answer to that first Great Mystery. The second Great Mystery is to try and understand the relationship between whatever you experienced and yourself. What is it that exists beyond you and how does it relate to you? Are they really separate entities—you and it? The answers to these questions will reveal more about knowing who you really are than it will help you understand the Other. The relationship between you and it (or her) is the second Great Mystery.

Create Third Degree Magick Books

Now that you have reviewed your second degree journal. Close it out and begin a new one. This will be your Priest or Priestess Journal. If you have kept up with writing in your previous journals, you should have no problem maintaining that practice. It is important that you keep journaling, and, at the end of your long travail on the sacred path, you will be glad that you did.

By now your BoS should be quite large and is probably in need of some revision. It is very likely that you have more information in your BoS than can be put into one nice collection. You may wish to consider separating your book into smaller books for specific purposes. One book can list all your spell formulas and incantations, while another can list all the steps, processes, ethical principles, etc., you have developed for the work of energy raising and magick. Another book can be your healing book, listing all the information you learned in that work, while another can be used for your divination work. You might also have a separate book to list all your readings with comments so others may learn from it.

Item 60. Magickal Books

Purpose: A suggested list of books to create, developed from the BoS.

Book of Ritual:	Lists the procedures for a variety of rituals.
Book of Magick:	Lists procedures for magickal work and spellwork.
Book of Divination:	Lists information needed in your chosen field of divination.
Book of Healing:	Lists information needed in your chosen field of healing.
Book of Symbols:	Lists common and special symbols used in work.
Book of Deities:	Lists all deities invoked—their traits and relationships.
Book of Devotions:	Includes all prayers, chants, readings, and devotions written.
Book of Readings:	Lists all books read with annotations.

As you can see, there are a variety of different books that you can compile. The Book of Ritual should contain the complete texts of all the rituals you may have written or found to be of use to you. The Book of Magick should include any procedures and principles used in that work. (If you do not do much spellwork, then this book might not be necessary for you.) Similarly, the Book of Divination contains all of your personal procedures and notes for divination work. The Book of Healing will contain your own personal results of experiments in healing, if you engage in this work, of course. The Book of Symbols should include all the symbols you have learned thus far, as well as any others you may have encountered. Feel free to include symbols of your own creation. This book might also contain any alphabets or writing systems that you use. The Book of Deities contains a complete listing of any deities you might be working with in your rituals. It may also contain other pantheons for you to review in case you run across another system that seems interesting to you. The Book of Devotions should contain any and all writings, prayers, devotional readings, poems, or other short writings that could be used in ritual or as a short devotional. These can be collected from other sources or written by you. Consider including devotionals for different times of the day or different days of the week or other daily events such as before eating. Other devotionals can include those written for the health and safety of family members, friends, parents, pets, and coworkers. You could include short devotionals for ceremonies when you do not have time to do a full ritual. These should include all sabbats, esbats, and astors, as well as any other ceremonies you practice. Additional devotions can include words to heal, protect the earth and its creatures, end social injustice, end hunger; words for peace, the sick, the dying, and the dead; words for alleviating stress, fear, and confusion; words to bolster friendships, dreams, partnerships (romantic or otherwise), a good job, a continuing or new love; and words to foster joy or gratitude. The Book of Readings should contain all the books you have read in your learning, along with a short description written by you of the book and its usefulness (a bibliography).

Create and Enact Personal or Group Rituals

As a developing High Priest or Priestess, it is important that you begin the work of writing and leading your own rituals. You have enacted some of your own or joined with others, so you have a good idea of what each is about and a general sense of the ritual procedures for each. Write a ritual for each sabbat, one for the esbat, and an astor celebration. Enact each of these by yourself or with a group in which you are involved, or begin your own small group for the purpose of celebrating these ceremonies. Be sure to take time after each ceremony to review its effectiveness. You may also want to consider doing at least one ritual (probably one you have done many times by now) from memory. This is an important learning tool and forces you to internalize your practice.

Each ritual should be a learning experience. You may want to ask yourself questions such as:

- Did I accomplish the goal set out for the ritual? Why or why not?
- Did I (we) end the ritual feeling energized and uplifted?
- What parts of the ritual worked well?
- What parts of the ritual did not work as well as hoped?
- What could I do better for the next ritual?

As stated, one of the goals of this level is to begin to teach and lead others. If you desire to lead rituals for others, you can adapt your personal rituals into group rituals by putting in some additional steps. Let's take a look at each step of the personal ritual and see how it can be adapted for group work.

1. The Preparation: This part will not be very different except that if you plan to work outside, you may have to give some special consideration to the conditions of wind and light. Consider ways that you can light and use candles that will not go out in the wind.

2. Stating Intention: For a group ritual, especially if there are going to be people with little experience in Wiccan practice involved, a clear explanation of what is going to happen and a clear intent are quite important. Take time to explain what each part of the ceremony will be and why it is being done. It is helpful to advise that people may participate or not participate as they wish. No one should feel pressured to do anything with which they may feel uncomfortable, and this should be clearly stated to all participants.

3. Banish and Purify: This step is especially important in a group setting and in a new place. The actual circle of people becomes the border of the circle of power, so the steps taken to banish and purify should be taken just outside the perimeter of the participants or they can be done within a circle of participants who are then asked to step forward after the circle is completed.

4. Raising Energy: This can be a very powerful part of the ceremony because you can harness together the combined energies of the participants. There are many ways of raising energy with a group. Some of the more popular methods are through dancing and chanting. Find or invent a favorite song or chant and have the participants sing or repeat the chant together. People may join hands or put their arms around each other for a stronger connection. Invite everyone to feel a connection between the people in the circle. Adding dance steps or movements can further enhance the feeling of connectedness and can be a powerful tool for raising group energy. Another great way to raise energy is through drumming. I urge you to consider studying drumming using a native drum such as a djembe or other hand drum until you can be effective in participating or leading a drum circle.

5. Calling the Quarters, the Layers, and the Deities: These are sections in which you can share the ceremony with others. Let other people call the four quarters, the deities, and the layers. You can share your words or let people use their own words.

6. The Ritual: Again, explain what you plan to do and be clear on how to do it so that others can gain meaning from the ceremony.

We can now observe how the standard individual ritual we have been using can be transformed into a group ritual.

Item 61. Sample Group Ritual

Purpose: An example for designing a group ritual.

1. Prepare your materials and altar.
2. Introduce the ritual and state intention (light working candle).

    Tonight we will celebrate _____ which is _____, etc.
    (Carefully describe what will be happening and why,

and explain that no one needs to feel as if they have to participate in any part of the ceremony in which they are not comfortable.)

It is I, (state common or magickal name)*, who comes before thee to initiate this circle of power for the purpose I state:* (state specific purpose of ritual)*.*

3. Banish and purify.
4. Cast the circle.
   a. Go around the circle of people clockwise and ask:
      Do you wish to be part of this circle? [response]
      Then ask:
      How do you come to this circle?
      (The traditional response is "in perfect love and in perfect trust.")
   b. Ground, center, and raise magickal energy.
      In this circle now we spin, a sacred rite shall soon begin.
      May we now be safe and sure for the work we here procure.
   c. Beginning from the East and continuing clockwise, set the four quadrants. Place ritual objects or light candles and say:
      Powers of the East, realm of the intellect, element of Air,
      we conjure thee—that there remain within this frame
      no adverse thought nor enmity. Hail and Welcome!
      Blessed be!

      Powers of the South, realm of emotions, element of Fire,
      we conjure thee—that there remain within this frame
      no adverse thought nor enmity. Hail and Welcome!
      Blessed be!

      Powers of the West, realm of the soul, element of Water,
      we conjure thee—that there remain within this frame
      no adverse thought nor enmity. Hail and Welcome!
      Blessed be!

      Powers of the North, realm of the body, element of Earth,
      we conjure thee—that there remain within this frame

no adverse thought nor enmity. Hail and Welcome!
Blessed be!

d. Call the three deities (God, Goddess, and Child).
Place ritual objects in the circle or light candles on the
altar and say:

O Goddess of the Moon, great feminine one,

bless this sacred circle and all work within it done.

O God of the Sun, great masculine one,

bless this sacred circle and all work within it done.

O Child of the Stars, great mysterious one,

bless this sacred circle and all work within it done.

e. Call the two layers (sky, earth).

O Father Sky above and Mother Earth below,

we stand in reflection to ask for your protection.

f. Place ritual pendant on self.

g. Bow to altar, announce circle is closed, and ring bell.

And now at last, the circle is cast.

5. Ritual.

a. Begin the specific ritual, and be sure to clearly explain
how to do each part and what it means.

6. Completion.

a. Release layers in reverse order.

O Mother Earth below and Father Sky above,

we stand in reflection and thank you for your protection.

b. Release deities in reverse order and extinguish candles.

O Child of the Stars, great mysterious one,
If you have come to bless this rite, we thank you now
for your bright light.

O God of the Sun, great masculine one,
If you have come to bless this rite, we thank you now
for your bright light.

O Goddess of the Moon, great feminine one,
If you have come to bless this rite, we thank you now
for your bright light.

  c. Release quadrants in reverse order.

   Powers of the North, depart. To your realm your light impart.
   And if intent and will are true, to this work you shall ensue.

   Powers of the West, depart. To your realm your light impart.
   And if intent and will are true, to this work you shall ensue.

   Powers of the South, depart. To your realm your light impart.
   And if intent and will are true, to this work you shall ensue.

   Powers of the East, depart. To your realm your light impart.
   And if intent and will are true, to this work you shall ensue.

  d. Open the circle. Ring bell.

   Now this circle we undo for this sacred rite is through.
   Let these blessings we bestow like a seed, take root and grow.
   For the good of one and all, Blessed Be!

7. Ground yourself.

  As above, so below.

This basic ceremony can be adapted for a variety of Pagan rituals and celebrations. Of course, you should alter the ritual any way you need in order to keep it fresh and interesting and to adapt it to different types of activities. Item 62 lists some of the types of rituals that Pagans or Pagan groups commonly do together.

Item 62. Pagan Rituals

Purpose: A list of some of the rituals that you may wish to write and enact.

Solar Festivals

Samhain:	height of fall
Yule:	Winter Solstice
Imbolc:	height of winter
Ostara:	Spring Equinox
Beltane:	height of spring
Litha:	Summer Solstice
Lughnasadh:	height of summer
Mabon:	Fall Equinox

Lunar Festivals

Esbats:	the full moon
Astors:	the dark moon

Coming of Age Festivals

Birth:	0 to 1 year
Maiden/Suitor:	14 years old
Mother/Father:	28 years old
Crone/Sage:	42 years old
Queen/King:	56 years old

Initiations

Dedication
First Degree
Second Degree
Third Degree
Fourth Degree
Fifth Degree

Life Events

Handfasting:	A ceremony of emotional commitment.
Handparting:	A ritual of ending a commitment.
Child Blessing	
Passing On	

Examples of solar and lunar festivals were provided in the discussions of the second degree. The other ceremonies may need further exploration here. The Coming of Age ceremonies are meant to honor the different ages within a person's life cycle and what that part of the life cycle represents. If you will recall, the Great Wheel not only displays seasons and sun and moon cycles, but the cycles of the human life can also be seen within it as well. The cycles of life are related to the phases of the moon and the four seasons. The moon changes from new to full approximately every 14 days. Approximately every 14 years, people go through a major transition in life. We can honor these human passages with ritual. Item 63 is a sample of a Coming of Age ritual for the transition between Child and Maiden/Suitor (14 years old). It was written to be performed in a group setting with different people taking roles for Center (ritual leader), East, South, West, and North. My tradition does not use the position of High Priest or Priestess for leaders of the ritual—these are simply degrees of training. Anyone can lead a ritual in our group and each is encouraged to lead it in his or her own way and practice. The person leading the ritual is called Center because this is the position in the circle that the person assumes. Others can act as East, South, West, and North, or any other positions that Center has prescribed for the ritual. This ensures that no individual person dominates all the rituals and we all are given the chance to learn from each other.

Item 63. Sample Coming of Age Ritual

Purpose: An example for designing a group Coming of Age ritual.

1. Prepare altar and materials.
2. Introduce ritual and state intention (light working candle).
    Tonight we celebrate the Coming of Age of our younger friends. In the Wheel of Life, we can follow the natural development of the human being in relationship to the phases of the moon. Approximately every 14 days, the moon changes from full to new or from new to full. This is a constant cycle of change and renewal. Each phase of the moon reveals a unique and fascinating aspect of the same planet. Through the moon, we also come to understand the aspects of the Great Goddess. From Child to Maiden, then Mother and Crone, each phase reveals another side of her. The same is true of the human life cycle. Approximately every 14 years, a person enters a new and exciting phase of his or her life. From birth, the person lives the life of the child, when all things are new and exciting. At about age 14, the child becomes an adult. The girl becomes a woman or a maiden and the boy becomes a man or a suitor. Both are ready for new responsibilities and seek out their partners in courtship. In 14 more years (at about the age of 28), the woman develops into the mother figure and the man becomes a father figure. The concept of father and mother can be as real parents or as

symbolic parents. They become people who are responsible and caring for others. Finally, 14 years later (at around the age of 42), the mother becomes the wise and respected crone while the male develops into the equally wise and experienced sage. These characteristics of wisdom and experience lead the sage and crone to their final years of life where others learn and respect their years of experience. The final part of the great cycle is when the person continues on to the next existence in preparation for the beginning of the next journey.

Tonight, we are here to celebrate the first of those passages—that of the child becoming the adult.

(Names:_____)

will cross the threshold from child to maiden or suitor. We invite all those gathered here to join in supporting and celebrating the crossing of this threshold of the life cycle.

Our intent tonight is to bless, honor, and support

(Names:_____)

in their passage of this threshold in the Wheel of Life.

(Light working candle.)

3. Banish and purify.

4. Cast the circle.

5. Ritual.

Please bring before us those who are coming of age this night.

(Participants are brought into the circle. They are led to the East part of the circle where two guards with swords stand. The two guards noisily cross together their swords.)

Are the children who come before us truly ready to pass through the gate of maturity?

(Participants respond.)

Are the young boys and girls before us ready to cross the threshold of adulthood?

(Participants respond.)

Then enter and begin a new phase in your life.

(Swords are uncrossed.)

CENTER: *You have professed that you are ready to continue on in this life as an adult; that you will always honor your childhood and be free to recall the joys of childhood living but that you will, henceforth, be called upon to be a responsible and self-guided adult member of the society. For you are at least 14 years of age and are ready to become a Maiden/ Suitor. Is this so?*

(Participants respond.)

CENTER: *Just as the new moon reaches the second quarter in its never-ending cycle of change, so you have entered the second phase of human development. You have reached the age of responsibility and expanding freedom. You are developing the capability to procreate. Your body is changing and developing into one of form and beauty. You are creating your own sense of self in the world while learning what it is that makes you unique. You are developing your own power and wisdom and are exploring new avenues of interaction and expression. These are all wonderful things. These are gifts given to you by the gods. But like all gifts, each comes wrapped in the cords of responsibility. Each gift can become a tool for joyous living or it can be used foolishly and can cause great damage to yourself and others. Ponder well my young friends these gifts. Use them wisely and you shall be rewarded. Use them foolishly and you shall have vicious folly returned to you in greater measure. (pause) If you are ready to proceed, we will begin the first walk of adulthood. Are you ready?*

(Initiates respond and are then led to East.)

EAST: *I will speak for East. Herein is the home of the element of Air and the intellect. It is from here that you gain courage and wisdom. It is here that you learn to speak the words that must be said and to be silent when silence is required. As East, I charge you to seek courage and wisdom and to express yourself as a responsible and caring adult. Do you accept this charge?*

(Initiates respond.)

For many young people of your age, the greatest symbol of adulthood is the car key. The car represents independence, trust, the ability to socialize, and the means to gain employment. Thus, I offer you a symbolic key as a gift from the East to honor your life journey.

(Give yellow key and move to South.)

SOUTH: *I will speak for South. Herein is the home of the element of Fire and the energy of life. It is from here that you gain passion and the desire to be with others, especially in sexual attraction. It is here that you learn the importance of keeping good friends who can make a positive impact in your life, while shunning those who may adversely influence you. It is here that you learn to love well in order to be loved, to pursue your passions when it harms no other, and to restrain your passions when a risk of dangerous excess presents itself. As South, I charge you to honor your friends and your loved ones, and to seek out the help and love of others when it is needed. I further charge you to pursue your passions so long as doing so will harm neither yourself or others. Do you accept this charge?*

(Initiates respond.)

I offer you this gift from the South to honor your life journey.

(Give red key and move to West.)

WEST: *I will speak for West. Herein is the home of the element of Water and the mysterious soul. It is here that you gain the powers of intuition and inner strength. It is here that you learn to honor and trust your own self even in the face of those who may wish to put you down. It is here that you learn to follow the wisdom and experience of your heart while still being open to the thoughtful opinions of others. As West, I charge you to trust and honor your inner self and to gain strength from expanding and learning from your own experiences. Do you accept this charge?*

(Initiates respond.)

I offer you this gift from the West to honor your life journey.

(Give blue key and move to North.)

NORTH: *I will speak for North. Herein is the home of the element of Earth and the physical. It is here that you learn physical strength and stamina. It is here that you learn to become strong and to push your limits when needed. But it is also here that you learn to honor those limits and learn that rest is as important as action; that silence can be as beautiful as sound. As North, I charge you to maintain the strength and energy of your physical self through good works as well as rest. Do you accept this charge?*

(Initiates respond.)

I offer you this gift from the North to honor your life journey.

(Give green key and return to Center.)

CENTER: *I speak for Center. Herein is the home of the Spirit and the Great Mystery that is the source of all mystical and spiritual yearnings. It is here that you learn to honor the mysterious and the mystical. It is here that you learn the essence of all things; to be humble and reverent in the midst of the unfolding of the mysteries of the God and the Goddess, the earth and sky, the sun and moon, and all life's many creatures. As Center, I charge you to fear not the mysteries of life. Take time to honor the mystical and be content to know that not all questions need answers. Do you accept this charge?*

(Initiates respond.)

I offer you this gift from the Center to honor your life journey. It is a chain that symbolizes the way in which one life is intimately connected to others. In it we place your other gifts and then close the circle—a symbol of the same circle in which you now stand.

(Put keys on chain and close. Place chain on participants.)

And now I address those assembled here. Fellow Pagans, family members, friends, and all others gathered here to support this person, I charge you to love, honor, and respect these new adults in our midst in all that may be encountered in their journey of life. Do you accept this charge?

(Response.)

Then, I present to you [Names:_____], *the Maidens/Suitors.*

(Response.)

She/He will now walk the circle and accept your congratulations individually.

(Initiates go to each member of the circle.)

6. Completion: Release layers, deities, and quadrants and open circle.
7. Ground.

This is but one of many rituals that can be created for a group using your standard formula. An example of a Dedication ritual was given on pages 33–35. Other types of ceremonies include handfastings (the Pagan version of matrimony where two people agree to join hands for at least a year), handpartings (the separation ceremony in opposition to the handfasting), child blessings, and ceremonies to honor those who have passed on.

Learn Advanced Techniques for Leading a Group in Ritual

There is more to leading an effective ritual: It is not just enough to say the right words, use the right tools, and follow the script. An effective ritual is magickal when it transforms the participants into another realm of reality. It is, in effect, theater—not in the sense that it is all false, but in the sense that emotions are heightened and people feel that something special is happening. I suggest that you study the principles of good theatrical production in order to make your group rituals special and meaningful for all involved.

Item 64. Techniques of Theater

Purpose: Apply these techniques to improve rituals.

- Practice.
- Relax.
- Be yourself.
- Get into your character.
- Keep the audience's attention.
- Be spontaneous.
- Move and speak larger than life.
- Maintain your principles and ethics.

These are some simple techniques that actors use and remember while they are learning and doing their part. Because rituals are part theater (though much more real in their intent), it will help us in our rituals to apply and remember these principles. The first principle seems obvious, but is often forgotten in the bustle of preparing a ritual.

No ritual should be done "cold"; that is, without any practice. It may not be necessary to go through each step with all the active participants, but, at the very least, read through the entire ritual and see it happening in your mind before it all takes place.

Relax and be yourself. This sounds easy enough, but, just like actors, you can become frozen in terror with stage fright when all those eyes are looking to you for guidance. This is another good reason to practice beforehand so that when you feel stuck, you can remember what step is next. Being yourself means doing only those things in which you believe and keeping true to your own character. This requires self-understanding, and no ritual leader can lead a genuine ritual without such understanding. One of the frightening things about leading rituals is that you are revealing to others your inner spiritual understandings. Be sure of them first before you reveal them.

At first, a statement such as "get into your character" would seem in opposition to the previous statement, but it really is not. As the one organizing and directing the ritual, you are taking on a role—the ritual leader (Center). You must determine in your mind what a person in that role should look, sound, and act like while still remaining true to who you are. If you are naturally a shy person, then being a strong leader may be a character part for you. Though a persona different than your day-to-day self may need to be created, as long as your desire to do so is genuine, you are not being false to yourself in creating such a character. We all have different characters we play in life: the parent, the child, the buddy, the sibling, the teacher, the student, the joker, etc. Being any one of these is not a false side as long as they are reflections of a genuine self. Define for yourself what the character of the ritual leader should be, and then work on creating that role for you.

If an actor cannot keep the interest of the audience upon the action of the play, then all is lost. In ritual, we must constantly keep all the elements of our activities focused on our intent. More than that, we must maintain the interest of our participants. Make sure that everyone there is an active participant in the ritual. What is often unfulfilling for rituals of other religions is that participants feel that they are not involved. Part of our philosophy is that all of us are part of the Divine, and that each can and should have an active role in Pagan rites. Incorporate chanting and dancing. Invite people to respond to the words "Blessed Be" and "So Mote It Be." Offer opportunities for people to take active parts in the ritual, and be conscious of times when people are asked to stand in place silently for long periods of time. Constantly ask yourself, "If I was a participant here, what would keep my attention and interest?"

Being spontaneous means being willing to go off the script if necessary. It means letting things happen and working with the situation to keep the ritual moving and flowing. Things happen; and sometimes the wrong things happen. Instead of fretting and worrying that the ritual might be ruined, improvise. If you forgot your wand, use your finger or a pen. Always remember, it is the intent that is most important, not the tools or the words or the actions or the clothes. Stay focused on your intent at all times and be willing to make instant changes, alterations, or revisions based on the situation at hand. Some of the best and most meaningful rituals I have seen were improvised (some purposefully, some not).

On stage, actors have to convey emotions and words to a large audience beyond their immediate surroundings. We are accustomed to speaking and moving with people in close proximity to ourselves. With a large group of people who are further away, actors must move and speak slowly and deliberately or they will not be understood. The same is true in ritual. Make all your actions slow and grand. They must be more exaggerated than normal movements. They must be larger than life. Try to keep your hands away from your body at all times. Your speech must be done in the same manner. You must strive to speak very slowly and fully. This is very important and so difficult—especially if you are nervous. Try not to shout either. Simply speak with a full degree of breath support behind your words. If you are nervous, a good way to calm yourself is to focus on your breath. Make your breathing full, slow, and steady. There is nothing wrong with taking a few moments to "catch" your breath. In fact, this is an excellent way to begin your rituals. Put this slow, full breath into your words when you speak and make your motions move with that same slow, full breath.

Maintaining your principles and ethics means simply to not do anything that breaks your sense of what is right and good. This means following the principles of magick and the principles of the Threefold Law and the Rede. Review all those principles before you write and enact a ritual, and make sure that you understand the impact and consequences of all you do in and beyond the ritual.

Beyond theater, a good ritual also incorporates music and dance. If you have not already done so, take the time to learn a variety of musical chants to use. If you cannot sing and do not have a singer to count on, use recorded music. Simple circle dances can be a fun addition to ritual work and, for large groups, drumming is almost always expected. Learn techniques for effective singing, dancing, and drumming so that you may add these elements to your rituals.

Enact Meditations

The Element of Spirit

At this level, you will engage in some very difficult meditations. In the second degree, you devised meditations for the four elements: Air, Fire, Water, and Earth. You will now do a meditation on the fifth element—Spirit. Take some time to carefully plan this meditation. What shall you do to seek out Spirit? How shall you meditate with this element? What does the element of Spirit represent to you? To what does it correspond? Answer these questions for yourself and then plan out a special meditation.

One possible way of doing a Spirit meditation is to stand or lie in a secluded spot and form the pentagram with your body (feet apart, arms pointed straight out). Begin by doing your usual ritual routine. When you have cleared a sacred space, lie down and spread out your arms and legs to form a physical five-pointed star with your body. See yourself as a star. Imagine yourself as embodying all the five elements. Concentrate on an image where you extend your body out in all directions until there is no separation between yourself and all existence. Transcend your human form and embody the element of Spirit. This, of course, is extremely difficult, but it is worth the effort. Even if you are not able to achieve such a lofty goal, making the effort may lead to some worthwhile insight. Give it a try and see what might happen.

Kundalini Raising

Another meditation is a continuation of your work on the seven main chakras. Having opened each one individually, it is time to develop a method of raising the energy of each in a continuous motion. This is known as kundalini raising. There are several methods for developing this ability. Movement exercises such as t'ai chi and spiritual dancing can achieve the same results.

One method is to sit in meditation with your arms in front of you on the floor or in your lap. Begin by concentrating on drawing up energy from the earth. Breathe in slowly. As you breathe, concentrate on pulling this earth energy up through each chakra. Think of the energy filling and activating each chakra center as you go. While you are breathing in, lift your hands and begin to raise them in front of you as if you were scooping up water. As you concentrate on each chakra center, your hands should be at the height related to the location of that chakra. Try to make your breath and hand movement a singular, slow, and graceful movement. Continue breathing in until you reach the crown chakra. At this point, you will have drawn the earth energy up through all the chakras. Continue to draw your hands up above your head and bring them together. Hold your hands in this position and hold your breath. Continue to concentrate on bringing the energy up through your body into and above your crown chakra. Then, release the breath slowly, and gently lower your arms out and down to where you began. Concentrate on releasing any unused energy out and back down to the earth. Try to do this exercise at least five times and then rest in meditation.

Learn the Principles of Group Dynamics

If you choose to lead others, it is important to understand the dynamics that are present within groups. People in groups tend to take on qualities that are different than their own personal qualities. There are many great books on group psychology and trust development. You should make a careful study of each of these areas to become an effective and trusted leader of others.

Starting a Pagan Study Group

If you are not already in a Pagan study group and are studying for this degree, consider starting a group in your area. Find a group of people interested in studying together and find a place to meet. It is important to meet on a regularly scheduled basis such as weekly or monthly. People tend to get confused and stop coming when meeting times are irregular. Give yourself some time before starting to advertise and drum up enthusiasm. You could meet just to discuss important issues related to being Pagan or you could start a series of beginning and/or intermediate classes. Using what you learned in your first degree studies makes an excellent curriculum for a beginning Pagan studies class. Allow others to share and teach through their experiences so that practitioners of all levels will feel welcome. As your group progresses, allow it to take on its own personality and unique qualities, and try to resist the desire to dominate and control the group. Always remember that leading groups is intoxicating. One starts to develop a sense of power and the greedy ego learns to enjoy exercising that power over others in order to feel dominant and strong. The emphasis in this path is on personal development while not forcing one individual's path on another. Your role as leader is to guide and assist. One who leads others with an attitude of the all-knowing is surely stuck in the road. There is no inner development of the person who gets caught in ego absorption.

Starting a Non-Traditional Coven

Another option for starting a spirituality group is to start a coven, but I wish to emphasize that the kind of coven I am advocating here is a non-traditional sort. The traditional coven is led consistently by one or two High Priests or Priestesses who take all control of designing and working rituals and directing the spiritual advancement of others. The tradition from which I came was begun as a reaction to this type of coven. I advocate the formation of a different kind of coven—one in which each person takes responsibility for his or her own spiritual development, but has a special small group where the members support and nurture each other. This is a non-traditional coven (NTC). An NTC has the following features:

- It exists only to engage in magickal work for its members and others.
- All participants have at least two years of training before being a full member.
- The working circle consists of only 13-member units.
- Every ritual should have either the physical or spiritual presence of all members.
- It meets on, or as close as possible, to every full moon of the year.
- At least one of its rituals is dedicated to community work each solar year.
- It does not contain the office of High Priest or Priestess.
- Each member takes turns officiating a ritual in his/her own way (this person might be called Center).
- No one tradition is made the official tradition for the group, nor is only one person allowed to dominate others.
- Any official standards for the group (such as any of these listed here) are open to discussion and revision by consensus according to the needs of the group and by using democratic principles.

The traditional coven used to take on both the task of teaching (usually in a degree system) and offering small magickal group work. The NTC does not engage in teaching. Learning should take place in the Pagan teaching group. Although many of these teaching groups include ritual work and celebrations, they tend to be on the sabbats and include large numbers of people, which makes sense. Sabbats should be large group ceremonies, and often these are the events that help bring new people into the Pagan path. However, these large groups cannot do the type of intense spiritual work that a small group can. In addition, it is difficult to get a group of people who are all at different levels of learning to be able to be involved in a complicated ritual. This is where the coven can be put to good use. I advocate that all members of a coven have at least two years of training (work equivalent to the second degree). Only after knowing how to work with these things on a personal level can one hope to be able to work with them in a group setting.

The NTC has the unique opportunity of providing all of its members with the chance to lead at least one ritual within a solar year. This means that all of the members of the coven are truly Priests and Priestesses in every sense of the word. This is the reason I suggest that the coven contain exactly 13-member units. (If two or more people wish to lead a ritual together, that would be one member unit.) This would ensure that all members or units would have the chance to lead one ritual during every solar cycle. Of course, all members will not always be able to attend every ritual. Here, I suggest that the person or unit that will be absent imbue their energy into an item such as a crystal, and have that crystal delivered to the group so that the energy can still be present for the ritual. In this way, the spiritual energy of every member will always be present at every magickal working. This does not mean that others could not attend the ritual work (others can be allowed to attend or watch beyond the circle), but I suggest the actual working circle consist only of those 13 units. There will be times when exactly 13 will not be practical, but I suggest that it be the ideal goal. If a coven begins to grow too large, it might be time to think about forming a separate group. There should always be room for others to observe or even participate outside of the main circle. This gives those who are curious, or those who are still learning, a chance to get a glimpse of what a working coven is about. Of course, you should only allow others to watch if the whole group feels comfortable doing so.

The coven should meet as near to each full moon as possible. Remember that full moons are often considered to last three nights, which should help provide some leeway for meetings. Of course, for some, it is easier to have a standard night of the week on which to meet such as the Friday night closest to the full moon. With each meeting, the person designated as Center would have the opportunity to choose what work will be taken on by the Circle and in what manner it will be done based on that person's practice or tradition. In this way, it is possible for people of many different traditions (even open-minded non-Pagans) to be an active member of an NTC. All types of magick can take place in such a powerful circle: healings, the needs of individuals within the group, the needs of others, peace work for the community or the world, etc. It is my hope that these types of covens will also see a need to do service work in magick as well as in the mundane world. Doing such work not only aids the community, it also helps others see the positive side of Paganism, and it is a great aid in the spiritual development of all its members.

A typical NTC meeting might include a few minutes of catching up with members in a light social way—especially if members only see each other once a month. Then, the group should informally form its circle and, one at a time, each member should tell about what has been happening in his or her life since the last meeting. This is an opportunity for the group to see to the growth and aid of each of its own members. The group should be willing to help any of its members with magickal, emotional, or physical work. After "checking in" with each other, the person who is the current Center or ritual leader for that night should discuss the purpose and methods to be used for the magickal circle. The group can then perform its magick. Afterwards, be sure to choose the next Center, date, and place to meet, and, of course, take the opportunity to do what Pagans do best—eat, drink, and be merry.

An NTC is a small band of brothers and sisters without overbearing parents. Wouldn't it be wonderful if there were hundreds or thousands of these non-traditional covens spread throughout the world—small groups of people committed to supporting each other in life and Spirit?

Stages of Group Development

The stages of development of any group, Pagan or otherwise, can be compared to the stages of an ongoing emotional relationship and marriage (or handfasting). Each of these are natural stages a group encounters when forming and then meeting for a period of time. Learning to recognize each stage helps a group leader (in a non-traditional coven, all members are group leaders) know the process of growth a group is encountering. Sometimes group members panic when an uncomfortable situation develops. Often, this panic is unnecessary, as all groups go through phases of growth and each has its related bouts of growing pains. If you plan on starting or leading a group, take some time to research the concepts of group psychology and leadership. The most important quality to develop in any group is the ability to openly discuss concerns in a manner that is fair, impartial, and caring for all involved. If this one principle can be a centerpiece for any group, that principle will carry them through all manners of trials and tribulations. Always keep in mind that the strength of a group is determined by how well it nurtures all of its members. Individuals in a working group must always consider asking not how their own personal needs can be met, but how the needs of the group can be met. This means that each member of the group must be willing to voice what his or her needs are and the group must then decide if it can provide those needs in a mutually beneficial way.

Item 65. Group Development Stages

Purpose: Be able to recognize stages of development in a group.

Courting:	People gather together informally and decide to form a group.
Danger:	Though many talk about ideas, few are willing to act on them.
Goal:	Push to commit to ideas, initiate a meeting to begin the process.
Commitment:	The people decide to meet regularly and decide on a format.
Danger:	Lack of focus of energy.
Goal:	Determine principles and goals early, remain focused on goals, determine steps and procedures to commit to forming a group.
Marriage:	The group is formed and regular meetings begin.
Danger:	Superficial bonding develops.
Goal:	Encourage people to share feelings, keep meetings flexible and open.
Honeymoon:	Initial excitement carries through several meetings.
Danger:	Look for signs of next stage of development.
Goal:	Keep energy high as long as possible, but beware of developing power grabs.
Disillusionment:	Power struggles develop.
Danger:	People begin to try and convince others of their way of doing things rather than focusing on group goals.

Goal: Remind people why the group was originally formed, promote discussions about health and growth of the group.

Forming a Partnership: Power issues are resolved and a period of stability is created.

Danger: Some may have pretended to resolve their feelings for the group's sake.

Goal: Continue to promote group and private discussions.

Working Relationship: The group learns to work together and maintain itself.

Danger: Though a stable time, the group may revert to a previous stage.

Goal: Constantly be aware of changing group dynamics.

Divorce: Members leave the group and the balance is upset.

Danger: The loss of members may cause hurt feelings.

Goal: Use the energy of new members to constantly renew and refresh the group.

Dealing With Conflict

It is inevitable that groups will eventually come face-to-face with conflict. As always, the important thing to do in resolving conflict is to be able to talk openly and honestly about it. Usually, a "group" conflict is not really that at all—it is often a conflict involving a few personalities within the group that are influencing others. Item 66 shows some principles to follow when dealing with group conflict.

Item 66. Dealing With Conflict

Purpose: Principles to consider when gathering to resolve issues.

- Once a conflict begins, be determined to resolve it as soon as possible.
- Gather together all those involved.
- Meet in a peaceful and appropriate setting.
- Let all involved be able to speak their feelings and be heard in turn.

- Discourage the use of blame and derision.
- Encourage active listening without emotional reaction.
- Try to find the emotional root of the feelings.
- Try to find a way to incorporate individual needs with group goals.
- Encourage compromise for the sake of the group.
- End the session with a resolution or accomplishment no matter how small.
- End the session as upbeat and hopeful as possible.

Learn the Principles of Advising

As you develop in your studies, others may begin to look to you as a guide and leader. Some may come to you for learning and guidance. If you are open to these requests, at some point you may also find yourself in a situation in which you may need to act as an adviser to another soul on his or her path. Of course, if this person's problems are extremely complex or if you do not feel comfortable acting in this role, you should encourage that person to seek professional help. It may be helpful if you have available information about Pagan-friendly resources in your area. You may feel, however, that you could be of some guidance with minor situations. If so, then you should study the principles of advising. Advising is the ability to help others find solutions to minor challenges. Learn how to advise others in spiritual matters without forcing your own personal beliefs on those who may not wish to learn them. Develop a positive way of helping those who may seek you out for help. Remember, what you can offer to a fellow searching Pagan is the kind of spiritual help that may not be available through others.

I must stress very strongly here that what I am talking about is informal and basic advising and not counseling like the type that one might get from a professional. I am talking about effective ways to give advice to someone who may have what appears to you to be a very minor problem. Under no circumstances should you attempt to do any sort of professional counseling without the proper training and guidance. If someone comes to you and needs professional help, then do nothing more than see that he or she gets such help. Attempting to do more than give friendly advice is dangerous to your friend as well as to you. However, most everyone gives advice at some point in their lifetime. The following suggestions are merely offered as ways to do this better.

Three Parts to Effective Advising

There are three parts to effective advising. These three parts are the preview, the discussion, and the review. Each is an important part of a successful and helpful discussion.

Item 67. Three Parts of Advising

Purpose: Steps to follow to advise another better.

1. Preview.
   a. Ask for a brief, general explanation of the situation.
   b. Assess if you are truly capable of helping.
   c. Express your limits.
   d. Offer other alternatives or people to seek.
   e. Prepare yourself to listen intently.
   f. Set out your goals and procedures.
   g. Confirm your confidentiality within legal and moral limits.
   h. Use psychic abilities only with permission.
2. Discussion.
   a. Use the principles of the Wiccan Rede and the Five Elements of Advising (see page 195) as tools to clarify the situation and find possible solutions.
3. Review.
   a. Review what has been learned.
   b. Review the solutions and goals to be enacted.
   c. Help the person see a solution through.
   d. Encourage independence—help them to not need you.
   e. Ground yourself.

Begin your session by asking for a brief explanation of the problem. Encourage your friend to be very brief, and explain that you just need to assess what the general situation is before deciding whether to continue. Be honest with yourself and decide if you can truly offer aid to this person. It is easy to get caught up in the wonderful feeling of being needed. But attempting to offer guidance when it is beyond your means can actually do more damage than good. If the problem stated seems fairly minor, then continue on with your session. If not, be wise and honest enough to admit that you may not be able to help and offer other suggestions or alternatives.

Express your limits to your friend. Unless you are a licensed psychologist, psychiatrist, or psychotherapist, do not pretend to be one. Tell her that you are not a counselor, but just a good friend, and be honest about your abilities. Let her decide for herself if you are able to offer worthwhile assistance. At the same time, do not assume that you are incapable of offering any advice. As a Wiccan Priest, you do have some spiritual knowledge and experience that you can share with another Pagan.

If you have both decided to continue, you may want to begin your time with some sort of preparation ritual. This may be as complex as having both of you create a complete circle ritual in order to provide a safe, open, and protective space in which to talk, or it may be as simple as doing a brief invocation in your mind in which you call on your deities for assistance and guidance. Concentrate on your intent, and prepare yourself to listen deeply and without judgment and prejudice.

When you are both ready, take a moment to define your goals together based on the initial explanation of the situation. These goals may change, of course, but it helps to have some ideas of the direction in which you will proceed before you begin. You may wish to explain to your friend how you will use the Wiccan Rede and the five elements of the pentagram to guide you in this session. If you plan to use any psychic abilities, be sure to ask for permission to do so before you begin. Also during this time, you should state clearly your intent to keep what is said confidential within limits. Explain that your wish to help her cannot conflict with your personal and Pagan ethics—especially the Rede.

Now you are ready to begin the discussion of the problem and the search for solutions. The use of the word "discussion" may be misleading. Many consider a "discussion" a situation in which two people share an equal amount of time of listening and talking. This is not the case in a typical advising session. In general, your friend should do most of the talking while you do most of the listening. If you do most of the talking, it is more likely the session has turned into a sermon rather than a time of healing.

The type of listening I am speaking about here is spiritual listening. It is different than the type of casual listening we normally engage in with others. Spiritual listening is when the listener enters an almost meditative state of relaxation and concentration. The words of the friend are the focus of the concentration. In the pursuit of the second degree, you established a connection with the mysterious divine presence of what we call the Goddess. Listen not with your ears, but with the ears of the universe. Offer brief words of wisdom not from yourself, but from the lips of that universal presence. This type of listening and advising is a spiritual act in itself. Specifically, spiritual listening includes the following techniques:

- Listen attentively from within your soul and acknowledge that attention with encouragements such as "yes," "uh-huh," "go on," etc.

- Paraphrase statements in your own words to be sure that you understand. Explain what you perceive from the person's words and actions.

- Summarize statements after a lot of information is shared to distill that information to some basic understanding. Allow your friend to confirm or correct your interpretation.

- Continually resist the need to make quick judgements and opinions.

Pagan Tools of Advising

As a Pagan adviser, you have some powerful tools and metaphors available to help others. These tools are the Wiccan Rede and the Five Elements of Advising as applied to listening skills.

Item 68. Pagan Tools of Advising

Purpose: Ways to apply Pagan principles to advising.

Use of the Wiccan Rede ("As it harm none, do as you will.")

- Cause no harm to your friend.
- Cause no harm to yourself.
- Cause no harm to others.

Use of the Five Elements of Advising

1. East (Air)—Sincerity

    Goal for the adviser: Openness and acceptance of the person.

    Goal for the discussion: Help your friend see the situation clearly.

2. South (Fire)—Subjectivity

    Goal for the adviser: To be able to perceive true feelings through words, actions, and impressions.

    Goal for the discussion: Help your friend get in touch with true feelings.

3. West (Water)—Soulfulness

    Goal for the adviser: Be true to yourself and your friend.

    Goal for the discussion: Encourage self-exploration to find the root cause of the problem.

4. North (Earth)—Supportiveness

    Goal for the adviser: Believe your friend is capable of finding solutions.

    Goal for the discussion: Confirm that you are interested in helping.

5. Center (Spirit)—Silence

    Goal for the adviser: Keep confidentiality within the limits of the Rede.

    Goal for the discussion: Listen silently with intent and confirmation.

Use of the Wiccan Rede is an important principle to maintain in any counseling session. You must be sure that anything that is said or done during a session will not cause harm to your friend, to yourself, or to anyone else whether mentally, emotionally, spiritually, or physically. This is extremely important to you and your friend's sense of worth and happiness. If at any time you feel that this may happen, you should end your discussion immediately and encourage your friend to seek help elsewhere.

You must also consider yourself. Do not allow your friend to cause harm to you or anyone else. As much as you may want to help someone, it is never worth risking your own mental, emotional, spiritual, or physical well-being, nor that of anyone else. Create limits in your own mind. If you feel it is necessary, offer a warning about those limits and explain that you will not tolerate any actions that go beyond those limits. Do not accept verbal or physical abuse. Crossing those limits means ending the session immediately. You must be willing to help yourself as well as others. Also consider the space. Find a space to meet where you both feel comfortable and that encourages pleasant conversation, such as a coffee shop or restaurant.

As the discussion progresses, use the principles of the five elements to guide you. The five elements are related to advising through five "S" words: Soulfulness, Supportiveness, Subjectivity, Sincerity, and Silence. Each of the five pertains to a goal for the adviser (what she should focus on for herself in order to be helpful) and a goal for the discussion (what she should be doing for the friend to encourage healing).

Item 69. The Five Elements of Advising

Purpose: A guide for effective advising sessions.

The Five Elements of Advising

Sincerity:	Define the situation clearly.
Subjectivity:	Examine and explain your understanding of the situation.
Soulfulness:	Maintain the session as a spiritual act.
Supportiveness:	Provide a balanced amount of support and guidance.
Silence:	Maintain confidentiality without causing possible harm.

Sincerity means that you are open and accepting of your friend. Withhold any personal judgments you may have about the person. Remember that each person must walk his or her own path and each will be on a different part of that path. Your goal is to help your friend see clearly where on the path she is and to see what may lie just ahead. This means looking beyond personal opinions and prejudices. Each one of us views every situation through the screen of our own opinions. Sometimes we even mask the situation to make it more or less than it really is. Listen intently to your friend when she explains her situation. Then, with short, nonjudgmental questions, ask her to define that situation as clearly as possible. Do not offer your own opinion of the situation. She must come to see it for herself.

Subjectivity means that you should examine your personal views. As you listen, try to receive as much information as possible. Much of this information will come through the words used (another reason to let her do most of the talking), but other information may be available as well. Be careful to note her movements. In particular, you may want to note whether her actions coincide with her words. More often than not, actions will describe more clearly the person's true values. This incongruence may be one of the difficulties she needs to face. Decide if telling her about what you have observed is worthwhile and helpful. If so, you may want to point out what you have seen and how it conflicts with what you have heard her say. Another method of receiving information is through the access of the psychic abilities you have been developing. Be open to any thoughts, feelings, or impressions you may receive during the session.

Soulfulness means that you should remember that this counseling session, as in all things, is a spiritual act. In all that you do during the session, be true to yourself and to your friend. Do not try to fake what you can do or who you are. Doing so may boost your ego in the short run, but, in the long run, it will only cause you or others harm. Always check yourself, your words, your thoughts, and your actions to see if they are true, helpful, and most of all, loving. Open up your chakras and stay in a place of loving kindness. Remember your ethics and the Rede. Be honest with yourself and with your friend (as long as that honesty causes no harm, of course). Keep in mind that your goal is to help your friend help herself. This is not a session to add to your list of wonderful accomplishments as the world's greatest spiritual adviser. Others will decide if you are a good listener and adviser. It is like helping a young child learn to ride a bike. She cannot actually learn if you hold onto the bike. You must let go and walk alongside only to keep her headed in the right direction and to keep her from falling. But she must be the one to do the learning and the riding.

Supportiveness is knowing how and when to offer the right amount of assistance. For most of us who are trying to help another, too much assistance is offered. We want to try and "fix" what is wrong, and, of course, each one of us believes that we know the proper and correct way to do so. This assumes that you are capable of "correcting" someone else, and this is simply not so. The only person we are able to change is ourselves. You must believe, first and foremost, that your friend is capable of finding her own solutions. If you do not believe this, then you will be constantly trying to impose your own solutions. To encourage this sense of personal healing ability, regularly confirm to her that you are indeed listening and that you are interested in what she is saying.

Silence is an important part of any counseling session. In order to create an atmosphere of trust, your friend must know that what she is about to reveal will not become tomorrow's gossip. Loss of this trust not only causes terrible harm to your friend, it will also destroy your reputation as a helpful person. But confidentiality is a tricky thing. Your first allegiance in a discussion must be to your deities and the Wiccan Rede. You must clearly explain to your friend that you will keep silent about anything that is revealed so long as what is revealed will cause no harm to any other person or creature now or in the future. Explain that you first must be true to your own ethics.

When the talk is obviously coming to a close, take a few minutes to review what has been discussed. Rather than just ending the discussion and then moving on, it helps to go over what has been covered. Go over what each of you learned and clarified, and review what plans your friend has made to help her make a decision or to ease the situation. Come up with a plan to discuss when these things are to take place and decide on a way in which she can relate to you the results of her action. Be willing to follow up with her, but only to a point. Remember, the end goal of your help should be to find a way in which she no longer needs help. Finally, remember to always ground yourself (and herself as well, if she understands and accepts the concept of grounding). Just as in magick work, healing, and divination, energy is raised in an advising session. Strong and hidden emotions may be brought to the surface and the stirring of emotions is one of many ways that energy is raised within ourselves. That is why it is important to always ground.

Begin an Advanced Study of Magick

Trance Work

Trance work is developing the ability to enter into an altered state of consciousness at will. The particular state of consciousness involved in trance is different than the state most attain while doing regular light meditation. It is a deeper state in which the body is so relaxed, it feels heavy and almost foreign. Some claim that their bodies feel as if they are numb. There is no longer any contact with the physical world. Trance is best developed through a focused mind and specific breathing techniques. One such technique is to slowly draw in the breath with a count of three, hold the breath for a count of three, and then release the breath on a count of three. This should always be with complete relaxation. When inhaling, breathe in warm, relaxed air and positive energy. When holding the breath, allow the relaxation and energy to spread throughout your body. When exhaling, release negative energy and tension.

In many ways, you have already learned to do trance work. You have been practicing meditation, which is the first and often the most difficult step. You have worked on aspecting deities and elemental powers. You may have already experienced a state of otherworldliness. Now we will focus on thought sensation to make a direct connection with Spirit and to find ways to access this inner power. Work on mastering the ability to enter into a trance state at will and with little effort.

A final but very important note on trance work: Though you may feel as if you may be connecting with other powers and energies in this work, ALWAYS follow your own inner instincts for what is true, good, and right. Never do anything that goes against the Rede and your own carefully crafted set of ethics. You are always the captain of your own ship. Always be in control. Reject anything that threatens to relinquish that control. Remember, you are always responsible for your own actions and their consequences to yourself and others. If this sounds frightening, good! There are always those who claim that they have committed unjust acts because another power directed them to do so. To act irresponsibly is not to act as a spiritual person. Like any other part of the spiritual quest, if you are not comfortable doing this kind of work, skip it.

Channeling

Channeling is the ability to communicate with Spirit. For some, channeling is the ability to connect with the life spirit of another person—usually one who has passed on. Though interesting, I do not recommend this kind of work. If we wish to truly learn and develop, we must try and get our messages from the highest source—the Great Mother. Working with human energies of those who have gone before is always a difficult and spurious task. It may even be dangerous. I believe we can sense those messages when it is necessary for us to do so, and deep trance work that connects us with those energies may do more harm than good. Instead, let Spirit work through your higher self and always focus your work on receiving those messages you need to grow and develop as a spiritual person. One method for doing this is called automatic writing. Enter into your sacred space and bring along some paper and a writing tool. Enter into your trance state and then pick up the writing tool. Begin to write. Write anything. Write gibberish, doodle, whatever, but keep writing. Soon words and images will come forth. Do not analyze or think about what comes up until later. Just keep writing. Later, when you have finished, read through what was written and see if there are any important messages for you.

Finding a Spirit Familiar

Some like to work with what is known as a familiar. For many, this is an animal companion in the physical world that acts as a teacher and guide. For others, the familiar may be something or someone encountered while in a trance state. These familiars act as guides and teachers for further learning. To contact a possible familiar, enter your sacred space and begin your trance work. Allow yourself to journey toward a special open space. Allow that space to become cloudy or foggy. After several minutes, look closely into the mist. You may see the shape of a figure. It may be a person, an animal, or another strange figure. Allow it time to come forth. Wait to see if it will speak to you. If it does, learn from it. Ask few questions at first. You may need to do several sessions in order to establish continual contact. Always remember that you are in control of the situation. At any time, you can ask the figure to leave—temporarily or permanently. It is your magick field. If this figure cannot help you in developing as a truly spiritual person, then there is no need to continue contact.

Initiation to Third Degree

You have learned a great deal and now it is time to recognize your achievements. First, review your progress of what you have accomplished so far.

Write a third degree Initiation ceremony that is meaningful to you. Be sure to cast a circle and implement the things you have learned about ritual and ceremony, including your meditations and the development of your inner temple. Mark the date of your Initiation because further study requires a year and a day of work beyond that date.

Congratulations, Lady or Lord! You are now a Wiccan High Priest or Priestess! Put a blue cord on your pendant and celebrate! You are now ready to begin work on the fourth degree.

Chapter 5

The Fourth Degree: Path of the Physical

- Number: 4
- Title: Wiccan Elder
- Prefix: Madame or Sir
- Color: green
- Gift: stone, incense burner, herbs, salt
- Goals:
    1. Profess a desire to continue study of the Craft of Wicca.
    2. Pursue the third Great Mystery.
    3. Write personal grimoires.
    4. Write about your experiences for others.
    5. Write your own myths based on a pantheon.
    6. Enact meditations on unity.
    7. Continue service and teaching to others.
    8. Continue healing and divination practices.
    9. Direct a community service project.
    10. Mentor or tutor a Priest or Priestess.
    11. Begin the process of seeking wholeness in your life.

12. Create and enact a ritual of rebirth.
13. Write and enact an Initiation to fourth degree.

The essence of the fourth degree is for you to be a respected spiritual guide for all members of your group and for your community. You now have the wisdom and experience to begin to record your experiences so that others may learn from them. An Elder is one who earns great respect for that wisdom and experience. Be sure to live your life so that you are worthy of that respect. As an Elder, you will be a representative of the Craft to your group and to the public.

The fourth degree is about wholeness and experiencing and expressing through the physical—but here the physical means the totality of the self in the physical realm. The primary emphasis is on learning to live your life fully and joyously while also expressing what you have learned mostly through writing (though any artistic expression would do) and through the final experience of rebirth.

The goal of this level is to find unity within daily life and to make your life a physical expression of what you have learned. It is often said that it is easy for a guru to be holy in the mountains, but it is not so easy when he or she returns to the village. It is time for you to return to the village (the physical world) and apply what you have learned to your daily life. Strive to find unity amongst diversity while still honoring the greatness of diversity. Strive to apply what you have learned and experienced to help yourself and others in the mundane world. Finally, experience the pure joy of living the Wiccan life! Earlier you learned the Wiccan Rede ("As it harm none, do as you will.") as a code of conduct. Now you can expand that Rede into a life goal that reads: "As it brings joy, do as you can!"

The Third Great Mystery

Hopefully, by this point, you have discovered your own personal answers to the first two Great Mysteries. You have discovered and sensed a power beyond yourself. As Wiccans, we call this power the Goddess, because that is how we best connect to this ultimately unknowable reality. We see how this Great Mystery is manifest through the energies of light, love, and life—what we call the Lord, the Lady, and the Child. Next, you explored the relationship between yourself and these energies. At some point, you may have discovered that the energies of the universe are also the same energies that exist within you. If you discovered the secret to the second Great Mystery, you will understand the statement that the entire universe can be seen in a grain of sand, or the statement, "As above, so below." You will understand the relationship and interrelationship between the microcosm (yourself) and the macrocosm (the universe). If you have truly delved into these Great Mysteries, you will have experienced them personally. They are not just concepts to be understood, they are realities to be experienced.

The third Great Mystery is to understand how these truths affect all of life and existence as we know it. How does what you have experienced change your view of all life? What is it that all things share? Again, this is not to be just understood; it is a truth that must be felt and lived. As you work on this degree, reflect on these questions and continue to practice in ways that help you experience these realities. You will be doing a great deal of writing, which will give you the chance to take on this sort of reflection. As you get into these higher degrees, you must be able to follow your own path of discovery. There are less and less suggested exercises because, by this time, each path is highly individualized. Be constantly open to which direction you should take on your journey.

Write and Create

The fourth degree is about putting your spiritual learning into a physical form, and expression through writing and creating is a great way to do that. In this part of the journey, we will concentrate on writing and producing physical works that express your spiritual learning to yourself and others. One way to do this is to create your own personal grimoires based on the Book of Shadows you have been working on. Writing stories, books, and articles, or using other expressions through words helps you to put your thoughts together in an organized and coherent way. It also allows others to learn from your wisdom and experience. Expressing your spirituality through works of art helps make your practice seem even more alive and joyous. It is not enough to just learn and develop if all that experience does not bring a heightened sense of joy into your life. The whole purpose of a spiritual journey is to learn to let the light within you burn brightly and shine on others. You can let that light burn brightly when you sing and dance, make works of art, write, or create in any fashion that is loving and joyous. Let's begin with a look at creating grimoires.

Grimoires are like the magickal books you have already created and are usually very fancy and personal. These should be made to look as neat and decorative as possible. You may wish to handwrite them and include special alphabets if you record information you wish to keep secret. But be careful to keep a key to that alphabet so that you can decipher it.

The term "grimoire" and "Book of Shadows" have often been used interchangeably, but I use the terms differently here. What I call my BoS is a three-ring binder with hundreds of pages of typed notes. It is done this way so that changes can be made quickly and easily. As you continue on your path, those changes will be made less and less often until you will be able to put together a more permanent book. That is where the grimoire comes in. This book should be a work of art that serves as both a reference and a monument to your studies. Take some time to carefully plan out and create these works for yourself. Decide how you will write each. What script shall you use? What kind of ink and paper will you use? How will it be bound? Will you use a premade journal book or will you bind it yourself? You could even make your own paper and covers. It really is up to you. The goal is to make books that are both useful and beautiful—a joy to read and a joy to behold. Item 70 is a list of grimoires that you may wish to create. Before you begin, make sure that you have revised all your previous books so that they will be up-to-date and ready to be put into a more permanent status.

Item 70. List of Personal Grimoires

Purpose: List of possible books to create for personal grimoires.

- ◆ Grimoire of Ritual
- ◆ Grimoire of Magick and Spells
- ◆ Grimoire of Divination
- ◆ Grimoire of Healing
- ◆ Grimoire of Symbols
- ◆ Grimoire of Devotions

- ◆ Grimoire of Gods and Goddesses
- ◆ Grimoire of Books

Also, consider writing for others. Describe your experiences and the lessons you have learned. You might write nonfiction self-help books, revise your previous Book of Shadows for public use, write texts based on your workshops and teachings, or create a Web page with helpful information. Set out a plan of what works you wish to write and then begin writing. You may find that the very act of writing out your thoughts may help you clarify them even further.

If writing nonfiction for others does not appeal to you, consider writing stories or other works of fiction for yourself or others. Try writing stories about your journeys, trials, and tribulations in studying Wicca or create a story about a fictional character and how he follows Wicca in his life. Try writing poems or essays. Be creative and have fun.

Unfortunately, much of our society's educational development involves writing things in which we may or may not have an interest. Thus, for many, writing can be seen as an unfortunate chore. Take this chance to rediscover the joy of writing. These activities are not for a grade. No one will judge them. In fact, they do not even have to be good. No one ever has to see your writings, if you wish. This is not about proper grammar or syntax; it is about expression of the soul. Start by finding a beautiful place where you can just listen to your soul, and then write what you hear in your heart. Don't worry about what you are writing—just write. Write and write and write.

If writing is not your thing, then apply the same principles to other forms of art: music, dance, theater, film, visual art, sculpture, gardening, flower arrangements, cooking, craft work, public speaking, making clothing, etc. Forget about titles such as good or bad, wrong or right, and modern or classic. Just create. Listen to your soul and then let it speak in whatever manner you choose. Create and create and create. You are the Child (life), you are the Lord (the light that burns within you), and you are the Lady (sharing your light with others in the spirit of love). Let your light shine for everyone to experience.

Enact Meditations on the Unity

In previous degrees, you meditated on concepts of perceived realities or energies as represented by the five elements. This particular meditation is a bit more abstract. This is a meditation on the one unifying force of the universe—what I call the Great Mother Goddess. She is the source of all things. She is all things and she is also nothingness. The two are not really opposites, but are the same.

To begin this meditation, begin your normal ritual for meditation. Enter your inner temple and get into your normal meditating position. When you are ready, begin to focus your attention on your own thoughts. Imagine that you are standing beside a railroad track and a fast train is passing in front of you. Watch your thoughts go by as if they were cars on that train. Notice the small gaps that appear between each thought just like the gaps that appear between each boxcar on a passing train. Try to get the imaginary train to slow down so that the gaps between the cars become wider. Concentrate on slowing your breath and entering into a deep relaxation. Focus on getting the train to slow down even more. See how the gaps between the train's cars become bigger as the train continues to slow. Observe these wide spaces between your thoughts. Try to get the train to stop completely so that you are staring at the blank space between the cars. See, hear, and feel the emptiness between your thoughts. Do not fear the emptiness, bask in it. Maintain your focus on that emptiness as long as you can.

If you can concentrate on this space long enough, you may eventually find that this empty space between all things is not actually an empty nothingness. It is, instead, the absence of a sense of separateness between you and all things. This is a way to personally experience what Buddhism and Hinduism tell us about the illusion of separateness. We identify with ourselves because our physical experiences reinforce this feeling of separation, but this feeling of uniqueness from the world is not the real truth. The only way to truly experience this reality is to go beyond the sense-self by concentrating on nothingness. How does this benefit Wiccan practice? We believe in celebrating the Lord and the Lady through nature and the cycles of nature. That practice becomes different and more intense when we realize that we are not separate from nature and the gods. Earth and all its creatures, the sun, the moon, and the stars are all really different manifestations of the same thing, and we are an equal part of that same thing. As it says in the Upanishads (an ancient collection of Hindu theological teachings), you are that, my friend, you are that! By knowing that all is one and one is all, one becomes more in tune with living and loving. We may have heard the phrase "all is one" before and it may have sounded like a quaint idea, but nothing replaces the experience of having personally felt that truth. If you can master this type of meditation, you may also be able to experience the truth of the third Great Mystery.

Service to Others

By providing service, we go beyond our own needs and see to the needs of others. Being engaged as a positive force in the world is part of being a spiritual being. There are at least three ways you may want to consider being of service to others: through healing and divination, through community service, and through teaching.

Continue your work with healing and divination. You should now be able to easily invoke your deities and raise and direct energy in your work. Be sure to write about your experiences for others. Train others as they seek you out.

You have assisted with other projects, but now it is time to personally organize and direct a community service project of your own. Remember that what you are doing is a spiritual act designed as much to continue your spiritual growth as it is to help others. Research what is needed in your community and organize a project to accomplish a single worthwhile goal. Afterwards, assess the success of your project and record your experiences in your journal.

Assist a Priest or Priestess on his or her path to High Priest or Priestess. Pass your knowledge and experience to a fellow student of the Craft.

Begin the Process of Seeking Wholeness in Your Life

By this stage, you have done a great deal of wonderful work and, hopefully, you will have made improvements to your life. There is, however, only so much that one can do on one's own. If you have worked with other teachers along the way, this step may not be necessary for you. But consider it anyway because some teachers only concentrate on certain areas of development. Here, you must engage in some intense soul searching. Ask yourself these questions: What are the qualities of a Wiccan Elder—someone who has great wisdom and experience and who can serve to represent the Craft to others? What do I feel I need to work on in my life in order to gain these qualities?

This is a first step, but I encourage you to take it further and ask others who may be able to help you to answer that second question. Consult other Elders and Ancestors. Consider past-life analysis. Consider divination work, aura readings, psychic readings, and other ways of exploring wholeness. Remember, though, that each opinion is only an opinion. You are a High Priest or Priestess in your own right and are capable of deciding what is right for you. Do not blindly follow others without considering carefully what each has to say. Also, carefully consider the experience and background of each one. You have chosen this path because you wish to blaze your own trail. You can do so with the help of others but only if it is your own heart, mind, body, and soul that leads you. Obtain as many opinions as you can and then write out a list of those things you feel you need to improve.

If you do not wish to seek out the opinion of others, then you can use the five elements to help you decide if you are truly balanced. A balanced Wiccan will have an equal amount of qualities from all the elements. Use the lists in Item 71 to determine if you have the qualities of a balanced person. If you find a deficiency, take steps to achieve that balance in your life.

Item 71. Qualities of a Balanced Person

Purpose: Determine qualities needed to develop for living a balanced life.

East (Air)

Self-image and relationship to self:
- Accepts criticism.
- Does not need to engage in self-pity.
- Does not see all situations as either/or.
- Is not arrogant or jealous.

South (Fire)

Self-control and relationship to others:

- Able to control temper.
- Expects no special treatment from others.
- Accepts responsibility for actions taken.
- Has patience with self and others.
- Works cooperatively.
- Enjoys success of others.
- Does not find fault or blame with others.

West (Water)

Inner emotions and spirituality:

- Does not worry unduly.
- Is open-minded.
- Accepts the virtues and faults of self.
- Has sense of place in universe (a positive theology).
- Is accepting of other philosophies and spiritualities.

North (Earth)

Actions:

- Able to deal confidently with emergencies.
- Plans ahead but is flexible when plans need changing.
- Accepts failure.
- Carries through with plans.
- Is not driven by greed or want.
- Does not engage in self-destructive habits.

Center (Spirit)

Self-worth:

- Able to balance activity with rest.
- Able to enjoy life.

As an example, let's take the first element on the list, Air, and see how we can apply these balancing concepts. The first item under the element of Air is about accepting criticism. You might begin by asking yourself, "Am I able to accept criticism well?" Take a careful and honest look at your life and answer that question. If you truly believe that you can answer yes, then move on to the next principle. If you are not sure that you can answer that question yourself, then ask someone else—someone you deeply trust and can feel comfortable in asking. Another way to seek answers is to consult your favorite method of divination. Ask your question carefully and be open to the answer you might receive. If you do find something that needs work, begin by simply writing down a simple statement, such as, "I am not able to accept criticism well." This simple act can be a powerful first step in changing your life for the better because it requires you to develop a greater understanding of yourself. The next step, of course, is to try and find ways of enacting change. Determine some small way in which you can make an improvement on each shortcoming you have identified. You could try to work on each item one at a time or you might put together a list of things. Write out positive statements of change that start with "I will...." In the example we are looking at, you might write, "I will accept criticism gracefully and without immediate judgment." If you have a morning routine or meditation, review your statement or statements before you end your session so that you can remember your personal goals throughout the day.

Remember to make this process a joyous one. This is not something to do to make you feel bad about yourself. It is about finding positive ways to make your life even better than before by seeking balance and wholeness. It is impossible to try and be the perfect person, but it is worthwhile to try and be the best person that you can. Even if you do everything on the lists in Item 71, you will still not be the perfect person, nor should you be—that is why we call it a spiritual practice. We walk toward a horizon we cannot reach, but we walk nonetheless because we enjoy the journey and all that we find along the way.

Create and Enact a Ritual of Rebirth

You have finally come to the end of a very long journey. By now you should be a completely different person than the one who began this process. Take some time to look back over your past years of development. Review your notes from the previous degrees. Recall how you felt when you began this process. How does that compare to how you feel now?

It is time for you to take a final and very important step in your development. You have worked slowly on becoming a Wiccan High Priest or Priestess. The only way to truly know that you are worthy of such a title, however, is to spend some time alone with the earth and your gods. If you are acceptable to them, then you are truly worthy of being an Elder of the Craft. This step involves spending several days in private communion with nature or your gods. It is a special ritual and a trying ordeal. It is both a ceremony and a physical, mental, emotional, and spiritual test of your strength and resolve. It is a ritual of rebirth in which your old self—the developing Wiccan—symbolically dies and a new person—the true Wiccan—is born. This final step is a very important one for you. It will take careful planning and a great deal of inner strength to carry it through, but it is a worthy step. Take some extra time to carefully consider and plan what you are going to do.

The essence of the Initiation ceremonies for the ancient mystery cults was, after learning the secrets of the Great Mysteries, to enact a ritual in which the initiate was put into a cave or dark place (the womb of the Earth Mother) and was symbolically put to death. After this ordeal, the initiate would then emerge from the cave and would be welcomed as reborn and a full member of the mystery cult. You are about to create a ceremony for yourself that will symbolically represent the same thing. You should plan on a spiritual ordeal that lasts several days. Consider including the following as part of your ritual:

- Eat only a small amount of very simple foods, such as raw foods or fruits and vegetables, or consider fasting, if it is safely possible.
- Find a secluded place or community where you will be undisturbed for several days, a weekend, or a whole week.
- Consider taking an oath of silence.
- Write a ritual to enact during the time spent.
- Find a group of close sympathetic friends to assist you.

This ritual will take a great deal of planning. The following is a list of steps you may want to consider in creating a Rebirthing ritual for yourself.

Item 72. A Rebirthing Ritual

Purpose: Help in the planning of a Rebirthing ritual.

1. Make a complete review of all you have studied so far.
2. Decide what you want to occur during this time. Read books on ancient mystery cults and Initiation, and create a plan.
3. Find a place where you can go for several days without being disturbed. Be sure to map the location for others in case someone needs to help you. There are many religious retreat centers where you can go to accomplish this goal. Find a place where you can be watched and protected but left alone.
4. Set a date. Consider it like a vacation. Tell others you will be gone and, except for your close assistants, tell no one how you can be reached. Check the weather carefully if you plan to be outdoors.
5. Gather your group of friends who understand what you are doing and why. Tell them your plan. Give them directions and information on how to reach you in case of an emergency.
6. Take a cell phone or other form of communication for any emergency and a first aid kit. Keep the phone turned off unless you absolutely need it.
7. Contact your physician or healthcare provider and discuss with him or her your plans. Make sure that you will not do anything that will threaten your health. This is to be a ritual death, not a real one.
8. Carefully plan how you will end the event. It should be as meaningful as the event itself.
9. Take your journal and record your experiences.

This activity is rooted in the traditions of ancient mystery cults. Although no one is sure exactly what happened during those secret ordeals, it is clear that they were meant to change the initiate through a process of rebirth. To experience this yourself, you need to be clear in your purpose. By reading as much as you can about other traditions and practices based on the same idea, you can begin to formulate a similar goal. There are many spiritual retreat centers throughout the country that are perfectly suited to help you reach this goal within a safe environment. It is possible for you to simply head off into the woods by yourself for several days and have a meaningful experience, but this can also be extremely dangerous. A safer way to do the same thing would be to have a group of like-minded friends engage in this ritual together so that no one is alone. But, if that is not possible, a retreat center where there are people that can look after you and assist you with your goal may be the best way for you.

Once you have devised your goals and have chosen a place to go, choose a date when you can spend several days without being disturbed. Discuss your plans with friends. Instruct them that you do not wish to be disturbed except in cases of extreme emergencies. Be sure to meet with your healthcare provider especially if you have thoughts about changing your diet. (Many traditions recommend fasting for several days, but fasting is highly problematic for many people.) Most importantly, make sure you record your thoughts before, during, and after the event. Item 73 is a checklist of things you might need in your planning. If you are going to a retreat center, be sure to follow any suggestions made by the center concerning preparations and equipment.

Item 73. Rebirthing Ritual Checklist

Purpose: Make sure you have all you need for your ordeal.

[ ] Place: ——————————————————————————
[ ] Dates: ——————————————————————————
[ ] Arrangements: ————————————————————
    ——————————————————————————————

[ ] Arrangements made with assistants or friends.
[ ] Had discussion with healthcare provider.
[ ] Plenty of water and appropriate food and drink.
[ ] Emergency communication and information.

[ ] First aid kit.

[ ] Tent or place in which to stay (retreat center, campground, etc.).

[ ] Bedding materials.

[ ] Blankets (take extra).

[ ] Medications.

[ ] Pen and paper, journal, or tape recorder to record your thoughts.

[ ] Ritual.

[ ] Ritual items:

[ ] _____

[ ] _____

[ ] _____

[ ] _____

[ ] _____

[ ] _____

[ ] _____

[ ] _____

[ ] Other items:

[ ] _____

[ ] _____

[ ] _____

[ ] _____

[ ] _____

[ ] _____

[ ] _____

[ ] _____

[ ] Ending planned.

The following is a possible plan for enacting a ritual of Rebirth. In this case, others who are there to watch over and guide him or her take the initiate away to a secluded place for the weekend.

Item 74. Group Ritual of Rebirth

Purpose: A guide for a weekend rebirthing ritual done with helpers.

Thursday night

Take a ritual bath and rite of preparation.

Initiate should wear simple comfortable clothes.

Check the list of items and pack (take no jewelry, cologne, or perfume).

Friday

9 a.m.

Eat a hearty breakfast.

10 a.m.

Basic rules are explained.

Initiate must agree to a vow of silence and fasting.

Hand signals for water, toilet, walk, and retie blindfold are explained.

Initiate puts on robe.

Challenge of the three mysteries is given.

Initiate blindfolded and put in car for long drive.

11 a.m.

After long drive, initiate is led on a long walk.

Noon

Ritual of purification of space and renewal is performed.

Initiate is shown to quarters and is given basic needs.

Saturday

Morning

Meditation and contemplation (no breakfast).

Noon

Initiate is given psychic tea.

5 p.m.

Vegetable broth and crackers for dinner.

6 p.m.

More tea.

Chanting and drumming through the evening.

Sunday

9 a.m.

Light breakfast is served.

Noon

Hearty lunch served.

Vow of silence ends.

Initiate discusses experience with helpers.

Initiate is asked to discuss the three Mysteries.

Blindfold is removed.

The ordeal is ended.

Initiation to Fourth Degree

You have learned a great deal and now it is time to recognize your achievements. First, review your progress of what you have accomplished so far.

Write a fourth degree Initiation ceremony that is meaningful to you. Be sure to cast a circle and implement the things you have learned about ritual and ceremony. Mark the date of your Initiation.

Congratulations, Madame or Sir! You are now a Wiccan Elder! Put a green cord on your pendant and celebrate! You are now ready to begin work on the fifth and final degree.

Chapter 6

The Fifth Degree: Path of the Mysterious

- Number: 5
- Title: Wiccan Ancestor
- Prefix: Ancestor
- Color: purple
- Gift: robe or other sacred clothing or accessories
- Goals:
  1. Profess a desire to continue study of the Craft of Wicca.
  2. Incorporate the truth of the Great Mysteries into your life.
  3. Revise and write books.
  4. Prepare for the end of your life cycle.
  5. Write your own passing ceremony.
  6. Tutor a High Priest or Priestess and Elder.
  7. Continue positive work for the Craft and the Community.
  8. Live your life in accordance with the energies of the sun, moon, planets, and stars.
  9. Write and enact an Initiation to the fifth degree.

The fifth degree concerns a continued practice for an extended period of time. By this stage, you are fully developed in your studies, but learning and developing will always continue. There are no specific requirements because only you will know where your path leads—you will enter the path of the mysterious. The fourth degree is really the final degree for a developing Wiccan. The purpose of the fifth degree is to simply recognize someone who has practiced for quite a long period of time and is to be considered more of an honorary degree rather than a final goal.

Although you may be quite young, this is also the time to consider what will be necessary for the end of this cycle of your physical self. Carefully plan and take steps to prepare for this so that you can put it aside and not worry about it. While you are doing this work, consider what death means in your path. Learn to embrace it as part of the journey of your eternal soul. If you can come to understand this, you will learn not to fear death. Do this work and then live! The goal of this level is to develop long-term ways of living and practicing a Wiccan lifestyle. This is the time when theory and practice must all come together.

Now that you have reviewed your fourth degree journal, close it out and begin a new one. This will be your Elder Journal. Because this degree takes quite a bit more time, it may be necessary to use a different journal for each year. These can be related to whatever focus you will be working with during the next 10 years. You might also consider looking through all your past journals. Consider writing a condensed journal in a story form that narrates your experiences. Make it an interesting book about your journey—a sort of magickal autobiography. Finally, revise all your grimoires if necessary.

Prepare for the End of Your Life Cycle

Consider those things that you will need to take care of after you have left this earthly realm. Consider how you would like your final ceremony to be enacted in a Pagan fashion. Write out that ritual and leave it with others so that it can be done according to your wishes. Complete the forms for a living will and related health initiatives so that you may choose for yourself how these matters will be considered. The idea here is that you take control of your life and its passing to other realms. You have worked hard to take control of your life so far. You have learned that you create your own life through your choices. It is time to apply that same principle to your time of passing, but doing so requires planning ahead. Do not shy away from this work. Plan out what shall be done with your belongings and your ritual items after you will no longer need them. Consult your deities and come to your own conclusion. Consider any other related actions needed to ensure a smooth transition, and carry out plans to see them through. Consider writing out a will. Consider what might happen to you if you become incapacitated or too sick to carry out your own wishes. Consider writing out a living will that will make clear your wishes.

Write Your Own Passing Ceremony

Now that you have done the difficult work of considering how your estate shall be handled after you pass on to another realm, consider how you would like to be honored. If you do not do this work, it is possible that you will be honored in a manner or even in a religious tradition not of your choosing. Write out a complete ceremony of passing in the way you would like it done. Consider carefully all the steps. Read the ceremonies of others. When you have completed your task, make copies and share it with those people you would most like to have in your ceremony. You may be thinking that you are too young to do this work and that you can put it off for later. As unfortunate as it is, though, the end of this existence can come at any time and you must be prepared for that possibility.

Teach and Work in the Community

As you have done with the other degrees, assist in the learning and development of a High Priest or Priestess and perhaps an Elder as well.

Continue to do work that improves those who may also be studying the Craft whether singly or in a group. Set out goals for positive ways in which you can help develop others or groups or covens you may be leading or with which you may be involved. Continue to do work that makes your community a better place to live for yourself and others. Encourage your coven members or students to assist you. Set out goals for continuing this work.

Set out any other goals you may have to complete during the pursuit of this degree.

Develop a System for Further Growth

With the earning of the fourth degree, you have completed your training in total. What lies ahead is learning to live your life so that it reflects your values. That's it! The fifth degree is nothing more than recognition that you have learned to live in this way for several years (I am recommending 10 years here). If you simply live a Wiccan lifestyle for 10 years or more, then award yourself the fifth degree. If you would like some ideas about how you can maintain a practice that incorporates all you have learned before, then read on about my suggestions for developing such a practice.

The Solar Focus

Ancient occult philosophers once believed that, when we are born, our emerging spirit passes through the realms of the (then seven, now 10) planets. If you will recall the discussion on astrology, you will remember that we are calling the sun and moon planets even though we know that is not really the case. To continue, each of the planets was believed to be a ruler of the sphere in which it orbited. The young soul would emerge from the realm of the stars and pass through each orbital sphere on its way to the earth, where it would then be born into the world. Each of these planetary spheres gave specific influences to the soul according to the characteristics of the ruling planet. For example, as the soul passed through the sphere of Venus, it was given its unique qualities of love. This is what astrologers do when they look at your natal chart; they try to determine the influence of each planet. According to these philosophers, it was a person's life goal to escape or transcend the influence of each of these planets and to return to the sphere of the stars where pure spirit resides. The analogy often used was of putting colored veils over the eyes until one can only see darkness. By removing each veil, more and more light is seen until all the veils are removed and the pure light is experienced.

For each year of the next 10 years, take a look at the separate veils of the 10 planets and try to lift each one by observing that planet's influence on different aspects of your life. By doing so, you will lift that veil and move on to the next. Each planet, then, will express a different theme for exploration based on the characteristics of that planet. If we were in the year of Mars, for example, the theme for that year would be to observe the many different ways that energy, passion, and assertion play a role in your life. Throughout the year, we would look at different aspects of this theme. We will progress by moving through the spheres, starting from the closest to the earth and progress to the farthest sphere on our way to the realm of the stars. Although we know consciously that the earth is not the center of the solar system, we can understand how the ancients came to this conclusion when we look up at the sky and see the sun, moon, and other planets circling around us in appearance. We will use this ancient model for our practice.

Item 75. The Spheres of the Planets

Purpose: Observe the planetary spheres of influence out from earth.

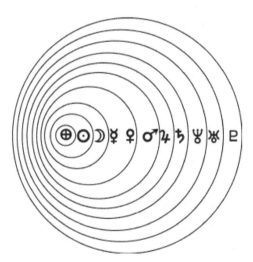

The Spheres of the Planets

To begin, we must know what each planet represents. For each year of work, we will progress symbolically from the earth outward through the planetary spheres. Item 76 lists the planets, colors, relationships, body parts, and keywords for each year starting from the closest "planet" (the sun). The colors are provided if you want to do something with a candle or other object to remind you of the theme for the year.

Item 76. The Planets and Their Correspondences

Purpose: A 10-year cycle for creating an advanced Wiccan practice.

Sun ☉

Color:	gold or yellow
Relationship:	father
Body part:	heart and back
Keywords:	the self, personality, outward appearance, personal strength, success

Moon ☽

Color:	silver or white
Relationship:	mother
Body part:	breasts, digestive tract
Keywords:	the emotions, instinct, nurturance, childbirth, motherhood

Mercury ☿

Color:	green
Relationship:	children
Body part:	lungs, arms, neck, throat
Keywords:	communication, the intellect, awareness, reasoning, short trips, creativity

Venus ♀

Color:	pink
Relationship:	lovers
Body part:	kidneys, neck, throat
Keywords:	pleasure, love, money, partnerships, socializing, beauty, possessions

Mars ♂

Color:	red
Relationship:	grandchildren
Body part:	head, face
Keywords:	energy, passion, assertion, achievement, sexuality

Jupiter ♃

Color:	purple
Relationship:	friends
Body part:	hips, thighs
Keywords:	learning, spirituality, values, fortune, expansion

Saturn ♄

Color:	black
Relationship:	grandparents
Body part:	skin, muscles, teeth, bones
Keywords:	discipline, responsibility, time, restrictions, perseverance, order

Uranus ♅

Color:	orange
Relationship:	enemies
Body part:	ankles, wrists
Keywords:	expanded consciousness, rebellion, nonconformity, idealism, freedom, creativity

Neptune ♆

Color:	blue
Relationship:	unknown people
Body part:	feet
Keywords:	illusion, mystery, mysticism, the unknown

Pluto ♀

Color:	grey
Relationship:	the dead
Body part:	sex organs
Keywords:	transformation, regeneration, rebirth, death, the subconscious

For example, the first year of this program of learning to live a Wiccan life begins with the theme of the sun, because it was seen as the last planet that affected the soul on its journey to the earth and is the first to be overcome on the soul's journey back to the realm of the stars. During that first year of the sun, you will be focusing on improving and magnifying the self (not in an egoistic way but in a celebratory fashion). During this time, you may wish to work on improving, honoring, or celebrating your relationship with your father. You should find ways to strengthen, celebrate, and honor your back and heart, and you should find ways to work on and pay honor to those things listed in the keywords for the sun: the self, your personality, outward appearance, strength, and success.

Now that we have a focus for each of the 10 years based on the 10 planets, we need to refine our focus within the year. The planet provides a particular theme for the year. The phases of the moon can be used to provide a particular focus for that theme. I call this process solunations because we are combining the cycles of the sun (sol) with the cycles of the moon (luna) to create a fulfilling life on earth. What better practice could there be for a Wiccan?

The Lunar Focus

For each full moon, we can assign a particular goal or ideal to our theme. We can use the powers of the waxing and waning cycles of the moon as well. Each phase of the moon has a particular quality based on whether the light of the moon is growing (waxing) or receding (waning). Each phase denotes when it is a good time for bringing something into your life (during the waxing moon) or when it may be a good time to let go of something that is not a positive influence in your life (during the waning moon).

Item 77. Phases of the Moon and their Meanings

Purpose: Apply energies of the moon to the sun and moon cycles.

Waxing Moon: invoking, creating, rising, growing
Waning Moon: expelling, restructuring, falling, withdrawing

The particular focus that you may want to assign to each full and new moon within the year can depend on which system of symbols and meaning you may be drawn toward. You can create any number of systems yourself, but I offer some possibilities here.

The Named Moon Method

One method would be to use the names of the moons you found or inscribed on your list of lunar celebrations. If, for example, you have named the full moon that appears in August the Harvest Moon, you may find a focus to your theme using the concept of harvest. Here's how the system might work using this method:

Year: one

Planet: the sun

Theme: the self, your personality, outward appearance, strength, and success

Focus: the Harvest Moon

Full Moon Goal: What can I sow or bring into my life?

New Moon Goal: What can I reap or clear out of my life?

The Astrological Method

With this method, you could apply a focus to your theme by noticing in what astrological sign each full moon and new moon is rising. By applying the meaning of that astrological sign to your waxing and waning moon, you can provide powerful meanings and goals to your practice. For example, if the sign of Aries is about being a strong leader, you might find ways to encourage better methods of leadership for your life during the waxing moon, while finding ways to be less of a leader and more of a follower during the time of the waning moon. In each month, the full moon will rise in one sign, while the new moon will rise in another, so you would need to look at the qualities of both. This method could be written as:

Year: one

Planet: the sun

Theme: the self, your personality, outward appearance, strength, and success.

Focus: the astrological signs of Aries and Libra

Full Moon Goal: (new moon rising in Aries) How can I develop leadership qualities?

New Moon Goal: (new moon rising in Libra) What can I get rid of in my life that would help me achieve balance?

The Tarot Card Method

The powerful symbols of tarot cards can be used to provide a focus for your practice. One possible use of the cards would be to only use the major arcana and to use these cards in their original order from 1 to 21, assigning each to a full and new moon. You would get a break at the end of the year because there are not quite enough for 13 full and 13 new moons, but, so be it. Another option would be to use the major arcana, but to randomly pick one card for each cycle, providing an element of chance and surprise. A third method would be to use the entire deck and to randomly pick any card to provide your focus. Here's an example of how this system might work:

Year: two

Planet: the moon

Theme: the emotions, instinct, nurturance, childbirth, motherhood

Focus: the tarot card—the Fool

Full Moon Goal: I will begin a new project that will help nurture children.

New Moon Goal: I will eliminate a childish habit from my life.

The Rune Stone System

Rune stones can also be used as a system for focusing on the main theme. If you use a rune set such as the Elder Futhark and include the 25th blank stone, you can use a different stone for each of the 13 full moons and for all but one of the new moons. Like the tarot card method, you could use the stones in their normal order or you could mix them up and use them randomly. To show the range of possibilities available for each theme and focus, I will give examples of how to apply other correspondences to the planets. Let us say that I have chosen the rune stone Berkana as my focus. One of the meanings of this stone is health. An example of how to apply this focus might be:

Year: three

Planet: Mercury

Theme: body parts—lungs, arms, neck, and throat

Focus: the rune stone—Berkana

Full Moon Goal: I will work to strengthen my lungs through aerobic exercise.

New Moon Goal: I will learn to stop smoking.

The Chakra System

Because we have only discussed seven main chakras in this text, using the chakras as a means for focusing your theme would require some expansion of the system. There are actually many more than seven chakras, so it would not be too difficult to identify 26. However, you could just use the seven main chakras and simply apply each one to two full and two new moons. You could apply each chakra to the main focus of the planet one month and use the second month to apply a focus to a body part or relationship. In the following example, I apply the fifth chakra to the relationship aspect of the planet.

Year: four

Planet: Venus

Theme: relationship—lovers

Focus: the fifth chakra

Full Moon Goal: I will work to improve communication with my lover.

New Moon Goal: I will eliminate all negative speech in my communications with my lover.

The Elements and Deities Method

In this method, you would combine the qualities of the four main elements (Air, Fire, Water, and Earth) with your understanding of the three deities (Goddess, God, and Child). The fifth element, Spirit, could be applied for the 13th full and new moons. As an example, the first month you might combine the qualities of the element of Air with the influence of the Goddess. If the Goddess embodies or represents to you the cosmic force of love and unity, and Air embodies or represents the mental side of the self, the two combined might represent the need to have loving and caring thoughts for yourself and others. Let us see how this might work out with our system:

Year: eight

Planet: Uranus

Theme: relationship—enemies

Focus: the element Air and the Goddess

Full Moon Goal: I will work to have loving and caring thoughts for my enemies.

New Moon Goal: I will eliminate all uncaring thoughts concerning my enemies.

The Mythological Method

With the mythological method, you could apply or invoke the powers of a particular deity to each moon phase focus. You would need to choose 13 deities, and it is my hope that you would choose only those with the potential to make a positive impact in your life and the lives of others. An example of the use of this system might look like:

Year: six

Planet: Jupiter

Theme: relationship—friends

Focus: the god Loki

Full Moon Goal: I will play harmless practical jokes on my friends to encourage laughter.

New Moon Goal: I will eliminate something in my life that impedes my sense of play

The entire process of solunations, then, would involve a commitment to working within a year's theme derived from the order of the planets and then applying a focus to the theme through the cycles of the moon. At each full and new moon, you should do a small ritual for yourself in which you determine your goal for that phase of the moon. Before the ritual, you should determine what your specific theme, focus, and goal should be. You may want to set out a simple chart for yourself listing these things. Once you have done that, you can enact your ritual and dedicate yourself to your goal. It is most important that you see this work as joyous and fun. Find those things that will improve and magnify the joy of living for you. It doesn't all have to be serious work, either. Add fun, spontaneity, and play to your life.

Of course, if none of these methods appeals to you, then ignore them or create your own. Maybe you would just be happy living the joyous life of a Wiccan and not follow some specific plan. As always, it is up to you. You should determine what is most important for you, but these suggestions may guide you to think in a certain direction.

Remember that, overall, your focus is to live your life the Wiccan way, which is a daily act of magick (transformation) and joy. This work should not feel like another chore to add to your life, it should be fun and exciting. Make it your own and find ways to make the system help you grow and experience life.

Initiation to Fifth Degree

If you have committed yourself to 10 years of continued study and practice and if you feel you have contributed to the life of others and the Craft itself, then you are indeed worthy of being considered a Wiccan Ancestor. The goal of this level is to develop long-term ways of living and practicing a Wiccan lifestyle. Do you feel you have accomplished that goal? Can you now live the rest of your life as a true Wiccan—with magick and joy in each day? This has been your goal from the very beginning, and from this point on comes your final challenge: to be a Wiccan in mind, body, heart, and soul; to be joyful; to be a person who shares and expresses that joy to others. So mote it be! Write a fifth degree Initiation ceremony that is meaningful to you. Be sure to cast a circle and implement the things you have learned about ritual and ceremony. Mark the date of your Initiation.

Congratulations, Honored One! You are now a Wiccan Ancestor! Put a purple cord on your pendant and celebrate! Continue to work toward truth and right in the name of Wicca and your chosen path and you shall be worthy of great respect!

A Review of Your Accomplishments

Congratulations! You have gone where few have gone before. Though many may talk about their religion, few actually commit a part of their lives to being truly spiritual. If you have followed this degree system all the way to the end, you will have gone through at least 14 years of intensive study and practice. You will, indeed, be worthy of being called a Wiccan Ancestor. Unfortunately, in our culture, being called an Elder or an Ancestor has negative connotations because only youth is honored. But remember that many earlier cultures gave almost god- or goddess-like stature to those elders who had learned the great practical and spiritual lessons of life. They were seen as wise and grand. They were sought out for their advice and guidance. Those who were called the Ancestors were spoken of with great reverence. It is time to reclaim that sense of honor for our elders and you shall now be counted among them.

You have been on a journey toward wholeness. Through the five degrees, you have finely honed and developed each of the four parts of the self and pointed them towards Spirit. Technologies such as telescopes and satellite dishes increase in strength when several are aligned together. Like the great telescopes that reach into the heavens in order to understand the cosmos, you have aimed the parts of yourself toward the mysterious One in order to become in tune with it. With the first degree, you learned a great deal about Wicca and spiritual development. The second degree taught you how to put that knowledge to use to create a personal spiritual practice. Then, with the third degree, you developed a way to help others through your spiritual practice and abilities. Finally, you finished your formal practice with the fourth degree by preparing and engaging in a rebirthing ritual in which you were reborn into a spiritual being. The fifth degree was an extended time for you to truly explore your spiritual practice as a fully developed and honored Wiccan Elder. Now, you have completed the journey.

May you truly be a blessed and joyous person after this grand experience. I hope you will share your joy by helping others to lead more spiritual and joyous lives as well. Blessed be!

Appendix A

A List of the Items

Appendix B

Books for Further Study

Chapter 2: The First Degree

Adler, Margot. *Drawing Down the Moon*. Boston, Mass.: Beacon Press, 1986.

Anand, Margo. *The Art of Sexual Magic*. New York: Putnam Publishing Group, 1995.

Angelo, Jack. *Hands-On Healing*. Rochester, Vt.: Healing Arts Press, 1997.

Barks, Coleman, trans. *The Essential Rumi*. San Francisco, Calif.: Harper San Francisco, 1995.

Buckland, Raymond. *Complete Book of Witchcraft*. St. Paul, Minn.: Llewelyn, 1986.

Campanelli, Pauline. *Pagan Rites of Passage*. St. Paul, Minn.: Llewellyn, 1998.

Cleary, Thomas, trans. *The Essential Confucius*. New York: HarperCollins, 1992.

Cooper, D. Jason. *Understanding Numerology*. Wellingborough, UK: Aquarian Press, 1986.

Cotterell, Arthur. *The Encyclopedia of World Mythology*. Chicago: Paragon Books, 1999.

Cunningham, Scott. *Earth, Air, Fire, and Water*. St. Paul, Minn.: Llewellyn, 2000.

———. *Wicca: A Guide for the Solitary Practitioner*. St. Paul, Minn.: Llewellyn, 1980.

Dawood, N. J., trans. *The Koran*. New York: Penguin Books, 1990.

Diagram Group, The. *The Little Giant Encyclopedia of Fortune Telling*. New York: Sterling Publishing, 1999.

Easwaran, Eknath, trans. *The Bhagavad Gita*. Tomales, Calif.: Nilgiri Press, 1987.

———. *The Dhammapada*. Tomales, Calif.: Nilgiri Press, 1987.

———. *The Upanishads*. Tomales, Calif.: Nilgiri Press, 1987.

Fielding, Charles. *The Practical Qabalah*. York Beach, Maine: Samuel Weiser, 1989.

Garen, Nancy. *Tarot Made Easy*. New York: Fireside, 1989.

Giles, Cynthia. *The Tarot: Methods, Mastery, and More*. New York: Fireside, 1996.

Gilkeson, Jim. *Energy Healing*. New York: Marlowe & Company, 2000.

Hutton, Ronald. *The Triumph of the Moon*. Oxford, UK: Oxford University Press, 1999.

Huxley, Aldous. *The Perennial Philosophy*. New York: HarperCollins, 1945.

Johnston, William, ed. *The Cloud of Unknowing*. New York: Doubleday, 1973.

Knight, Sirona. The Little Giant Encyclopedia of Runes. New York: Sterling Publishing, 2000.

Krieger, Dolores. *The Therapeutic Touch*. Upper Saddle River, N.J.: Prentice Hall, 1979.

Meadows, Kenneth. *Rune Power*. Dorset, UK: Element Books Ltd., 1996.

————. *The Shamanic Experience*. Dorset, UK: Element Books, 1991.

Morrison, Dorothy. *Everyday Magic*. St. Paul, Minn.: Llewellyn, 1998.

Neihardt, John G. *Black Elk Speaks*. Nebr.: University of Nebraska Press, 1979.

Pajeon, Kala, and Ketz Pajeon. *Candle Magick Workbook*. Sacramento, Calif.: Citadel Press, 1991.

Parker, Julia. *The Astrologer's Handbook*. UK: Chancellor Press, 1995.

Pennick, Nigel. *Magical Alphabets*. York Beach, Maine: Samuel Weiser, 1992.

Powell, Tag, and Judith Powell. *Taming the Wild Pendulum*. Fla.: Top of the Mountain Publishing, 1995.

Reif, Jennifer. *The Mysteries of Demeter*. York Beach, Maine: Samuel Weiser, 1999.

Rodway, Marie. *A Wiccan Herbal*. Slough, UK: W. Foulsham & Co., 1997.

Schirner, Markus. *Pendulum Workbook*. New York: Sterling Publishing, 1999.

Starhawk. *The Spiral Dance*. New York: HarperCollins, 1989.

Telesco, Patricia. *The Wiccan Book of Ceremonies and Rituals*. Sacramento, Calif.: Citadel Press, 1998.

Tyson, Donald. *Ritual Magic: What It Is and How To Do It*. St. Paul, Minn.: Llewellyn, 1997.

Chapter 3: The Second Degree

Andrews, Ted. *How to Develop and Use Psychic Touch*. St. Paul, Minn.: Llewellyn, 1999.

Bloom, William. *Psychic Protection*. UK: Piatkus, 1996.

Choquette, Sonia. *The Psychic Pathway: A Workbook for Reawakening the Voice of Your Soul*. New York: Three Rivers Press, 1994.

Diemer, Deedre. *The ABCs of Chakra Therapy*. York Beach, Maine: Samuel Weiser, 1998.

Humphrey, Naomi. *Meditation: The Inner Way*. Wellingborough, UK: Aquarian Press, 1987.

Levey, Joel, and Michelle Levey. *The Fine Arts of Relaxation, Concentrations, and Meditation*. Boston: Wisdom Publications, 1991.

Chapter 4: The Third Degree

Carnes, Robin Deen, and Sally Craig. *Sacred Circles: A Guide to Creating Your Own Women's Spirituality Group*. New York: HarperCollins, 1998.

Cuningham, Scott. *Living Wicca*. St. Paul, Minn.: Llewellyn, 2000.

Grey Cat. *Deepening Witchcraft*. Toronto, Canada: ECW Press, 2002.

Harrow, Judy. *Spiritual Mentoring*. Toronto, Canada: ECW Press, 2002.

———. *Wicca Covens: How to Start and Organize Your Own*. Sacramento, Calif.: Citadel Press, 1999.

Shaffer, Carolyn R., and Kristin Anundsen. *Creating Community Anywhere*. New York: Tarcher Putnam Books, 1993.

Telesco, Patricia. *Advanced Wicca*. Sacramento, Calif.: Citadel Press, 2000.

Index

About the Author

Shanddaramon is a creative artist who works as a director of music and arts at a Unitarian-Universalist church. Shanddaramon is also a brother in the Sacred Order of Living Paganism—a spiritual order of men and women promoting Pagan learning, practice, and service. He is a published writer, composer, and poet, and teaches others in the ways of connecting a life of spirit to the arts. He has often sought ways in which to combine his interest in the arts with a growing interest in the mystical and, specifically, through Paganism. He applies these skills through his art and writing and through services such as divinatory advising, pastoral counseling, and ritual work. Combining the arts with mysticism, he has created classes and workshops for others with similar interests and currently leads a Pagan studies class. He can be contacted at mail@shanddaramon.com.